CRIMES AND CRIMINALS

Monstrous Murders and Evil Deeds

BLITZ EDITIONS

Published by Blitz Editions
an imprint of Bookmart Ltd
Registered Number 2372865
Trading as Bookmart Ltd
Desford Road
Enderby
Leicester LE9 5AD

ISBN 1 85605 100 5

This material has previously appeared in *Strange But True*

Thanks to the Hulton Picture Company and
Mary Evans Picture Library for sourcing pictures.

50929

CRIMES
AND
CRIMINALS

LORD LUCAN
The Vanishing Peer

What happened to Lord Lucan? On a November night in 1974, the gambler earl murdered his children's nanny, attacked his wife – and has never been seen again

The door of the crowded saloon bar of the Plumbers Arms burst open and an hysterical, bloodstained woman stumbled in. 'Help me,' she sobbed. 'Help me. I have just escaped from a murderer. My children...my children. He's in the house.

'He's murdered the nanny.'

The distraught woman was too upset to reveal much more. Barman Arthur Whitehouse sat her down while his wife dabbed a wet towel at the deep gash on her face. The woman was wearing a rain-sodden dress and no shoes.

They called an ambulance and she was taken to the St George's Hospital while police went to her home nearby. It was a five-storey Georgian house, 46 Lower Belgrave Street in Belgravia, one of the most exclusive streets in London. For this was no ordinary victim of crime. The sobbing woman was Veronica, wife of the heir to one of the most aristocratic families in England. Her husband, by now on the run, was Richard John Bingham - better known as Lord Lucan.

'Help me. I have just escaped from a murderer...He's murdered the nanny'

When two policemen forced their way into Lady Lucan's house it was largely in darkness. Sergeant Donald Baker flashed his torch down the hallway and noticed bloodstains on the wall at the far end.

He and his colleague warily ascended a flight of stairs leading to a half-landing. In the dim light they noticed a pool of blood next to a door leading to the

Above: *Lady Lucan's doctor visits her palatial Belgravia home, 46 Lower Belgrave Street, where the attack took place.*

Left: *Lady Lucan leaves home to attend the inquest into the death of her children's nanny.*

Opposite: *Lord Richard John Bingham (later to inherit the title Lord Lucan) marries army major's daughter Veronica Duncan on 28 November 1963.*

breakfast room. Two or three bloodied footprints were evident. They continued to the second floor. Peering into one of the bedrooms, the officers noticed a bloodstained towel lying on a double bed.

Climbing further stairs, they found the sole remaining occupants of the house - a little boy and girl asleep in their nursery. Yet another door revealed an older child, Lady Frances Lucan, staring wide-eyed, and dressed in her pyjamas.

The last part of the house they visited was the basement. There the policemen found a large canvas mailbag containing the body of the children's nanny. She was twenty-nine-year-old Sandra Rivett, mother of a young child, and like Lady Lucan separated from her husband. She had been brutally battered to death.

Of the Seventh Lord Lucan there was no sign. Apart from one brief encounter that night, he was never seen again.

LADY LUCAN TELLS HER TALE

Meanwhile, in her hospital bed, Lady Lucan was telling her version of events of the night of 7 November 1974. Talking painfully through the bruising on her face and the lacerations to her scalp, she recalled how the evening had started. She had been sitting quietly at home with her children. Also at home was the nanny, Sandra. She had originally been given the evening off. Instead, at the last minute, she decided to stay in the house.

She couldn't recognize the figure, but she knew the voice of her attacker - it was that of her estranged husband

---

At around nine o'clock Sandra popped her head round the door of Lady Lucan's room and offered to make a cup of tea. Over twenty minutes later, when the nanny had not returned, Lady Lucan decided to find out what was wrong.

She walked down to the basement kitchen and saw in front of her the shadowy figure of a man crouched over a shapeless form on the floor. It was the body of Sandra Rivett and the intruder was trying to bundle her lifeless form into a canvas mailbag. Lady Lucan screamed out. She stopped only when the

Above: *Divers search for Lord Lucan's body in Newhaven harbour, close to where his car was found after his drive from London.*

Right: *Police dogs used at Newhaven in the hunt for Lucan, the peer who vanished without trace, sight – or scent.*

man turned his attention to her, beating her badly around the face and head.

She could not recognize the figure in the dim light but she told police officers afterwards that the voice she heard was that of her estranged husband. Yet, curiously, as Lady Lucan lay trembling moments later on her bed, it was her husband who was at her side trying to comfort her.

HUNTING THE RUNAWAY LORD

A huge manhunt was immediately launched. Police first checked his rented flat, a short walk away at 72a Elizabeth Street. The earl's Mercedes car was parked outside. Inside a suit, spectacles, a wallet and keys were neatly laid out on the bed. Police also found his passport.

The first police checks were completed within two hours. But by then Lord Lucan was 50 miles away - steering a borrowed Ford Corsair into the drive of the house of friends, Ian and Susan Maxwell Scott, at Uckfield, Sussex. It was then that he told his side of the story.

He said he had been walking past the family home en route to his own flat to change for dinner. Through the blinds of the basement window he spotted what appeared to be a man attacking his wife.

Through the blinds Lucan said he saw a man attacking his wife: 'I let myself in...and dashed down to protect her'

He said: 'I let myself in with my own key and dashed down to protect her. But I slipped on a pool of blood and the attacker ran off. My wife was hysterical and accused me of being the attacker.'

One other person who heard from Lucan that night - his mother, the Dowager Countess of Lucan. He telephoned her and told her there had been a 'terrible catastrophe' at the family home. He reported that his wife had been hurt and the nanny injured. He asked his mother to collect the children.

There was one further call to the Dowager Lady Lucan. It came just after midnight as she stood with a police officer by her side. Lucan again asked about his children and was asked by his mother: 'Look, the police are here - do you want to speak to them?' Her son told her: 'I will ring them in the morning, and I will ring you too.' Then he rang off.

The eldest child, Lady Frances, was also questioned. She said she had been watching television with her mother when nanny Sandra popped in to offer to make them tea. When this failed to arrive, her mother went down to look for the nanny and shortly afterwards Frances heard a scream. Her mother reappeared with blood on her face, followed into the bedroom by her father.

BATTLING IN THE BASEMENT

The following day, a more lucid Lady Lucan sat up in her hospital bed. She said that she had found the kitchen in darkness and called out Sandra's name. Hearing a sound behind her she turned but was struck on the head with a heavy instrument. She claimed that her attacker tried to force his fingers down her throat and into her eyes. He only let go when she grabbed his private parts. She then calmed her husband and went with him upstairs. When he left their bedroom, she had raced out and raised the alarm.

The weapon used in the attack had been recovered early in the hunt. It was a length of lead piping wrapped in hospital sticking plaster. It was found covered in blood beside some broken crockery. The debris revealed how the terrifed Sandra had dropped the cups and saucers when she was attacked in the darkness.

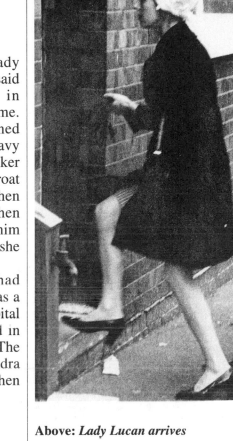

Above: *Lady Lucan arrives at Westminster Coroner's Court following her husband's disappearance.*

Left: *Roger Rivett, estranged husband of murdered nanny Sandra, arrives for the inquest on his wife.*

Two policemen who were to pursue the Lucan case for years afterwards - Detective Superintendent Roy Ranson, head of the local CID, and his deputy Detective Inspector David Gerring - launched a nationwide hunt.

They found the weapon - a length of lead piping covered in Sandra's blood

---

All ports and airports were alerted. But the alarm was futile. For the day after the murder, Lord Lucan's borrowed car was abandoned at Newhaven in Sussex. In it was part of the lead pipe used to batter Sandra Rivett to death.

Police also began a check of the fugitive peer's friends in Britain. They suspected that rich and aristocratic associates might be hiding him. But the more they dug into the lifestyle of the Lucans, the greater the mystery.

Below: *Lord Lucan's mother, the Dowager Countess, whom her son telephoned while on the run.*

A FAILED MARRIAGE

Pert, blonde Veronica Duncan had married Lord Bingham on 28 November 1963. Veronica, twenty-six, was an Army major's daughter who had done some modelling. Her husband, then Lord Bingham, was socially her 'superior'. Educated at Eton, he had served in the Coldstream Guards and worked in the City. But in 1960 he became a professional gambler. Less than a year after their marriage, Lucan's father died and he inherited his title and land.

Bankruptcy loomed, and Lucan blamed his wife for all his troubles

---

The marriage lasted only 10 years, however. The couple separated in 1974 at a time when Lord Lucan was spending all afternoon and every evening in the gambling clubs of London's West End. He fought for the custody of his children but lost. He even resorted to snatching two of them while they were out with their nanny. He was forced by a court to return them. He spied on Lady Lucan, and tried to commit her to a mental institution. Meanwhile, his gambling debts mounted. Bankruptcy loomed. He blamed his wife for all his troubles.

Yet on the evening of the murder, he did not seem to be acting abnormally. He left his flat in the morning to buy a book on Greek shipping tycoons and then went to lunch at the Clermont Club. Later, he met a friend before returning to the Clermont at about 8.45pm. He booked dinner for four at 10.30. The friends arrived but Lucan didn't.

The next person to see the fugitive peer was Susan Maxwell Scott. That night her husband was staying in London and she was alone at their grand home, Grants Hill House, Uckfield, Sussex. Lucan arrived at around midnight and awoke her. Susan Maxwell Scott told Ranson that Lord Lucan was somewhat dishevelled. She gave him a scotch as he told her his version of the night's horrific events. He made a phone call to his mother and he wrote some letters. He then left at about 1.15am saying that he was 'going back' to London.

WHAT HAPPENED TO 'LUCKY LUKE'?

The letters were sent to another friend, Bill Shand Kydd. One, headed 'financial matters', referred to a sale of family silver. In the other, Lucan wrote: 'The most ghastly circumstances arose tonight ... when I interrupted the fight at Lower Belgrave Street and a man left. Veronica accused me of having hired him...

'Veronica has demonstrated a hatred for me in the past,' Lucan wrote to a friend

'The circumstantial evidence is strong in that Veronica will say that it is all my doing and I will lie doggo for a while, but I am only concerned about the children. If you could manage it I would like them to live with you. Veronica has demonstrated a hatred for me in the past and would do anything to see me accused. For George and Frances to go through life knowing their father had been in the dock accused of attempted murder would be too much for them...'

Both letters were signed 'Lucky'.

The two letters were the last word in the hunt for the vanishing lord. It was a search that spread abroad with reports of sightings in Australia, North America and southern Africa.

A year after his disappearance, a coroner's inquest investigated Sandra Rivett's death. Its finding was Murder. And, unusually in British law, Lord Lucan was named as the murderer.

Left: *Lady Lucan and her husband split up in 1974, largely because of his lifestyle around the gambling clubs of London.*

Below: *Lady Lucan's marriage lasted only ten years. She was left with the custody of their son and two daughters.*

So what happened to Richard John Bingham, Seventh Earl of Lucan, Baron Bingham of Castlebar, Baron Bingham of Melcombe, baronet of Nova Scotia, known to his family as John, to his friends as Johnny or Luke, and to his gaming table associates as 'Lucky'?

Although both of them since retired from Scotland Yard, the two policemen who led the search expressed strong yet differing views about the fate of their quarry. David Gerring believes: 'Lucan is still in hiding somewhere and he is the only man who knows the full story. He is a lord and he is still a gentleman and he is still gambling on the odds that no one will ever find him.' Roy Ranson maintains: 'Lucan killed the nanny by mistake, thinking he could dispose of his wife and get custody of the children he loved. When he realized his error, he killed himself in some remote spot like a lord and gentleman.'

ADOLF EICHMANN
Nazi War Criminal

Adolf Eichmann left school at fifteen without qualifications. Looking for a purpose in life, he joined the infant Nazi party and found it: the extermination of 6 million Jews in the death camps of wartime Europe

The Holocaust stands as the most monumental crime in history - the systematic extermination of 6 million Jews and the murders of a further 6 million Russians, Poles, gypsies, homosexuals and other 'inferiors' who threatened Adolf Hitler's warped vision of a racially pure world dominated by his cruel stormtroopers.

The vanquished races died at the hands of unspeakably evil men - drunken Lithuanian quislings in the conquered eastern territories who machine-gunned their victims into lime pits; brutish *Volksdeutsche* [ethnic Germans] from Poland and Czechoslovakia who dropped the gas into the chambers of Auschwitz

Above: *Bullet-proof glass is used in the making of the 'cabin' in which Eichmann would face trial.*

Opposite: *Adolf Eichmann was the ice-cold officer who put his leader Hitler's maniacal holocaust into effect.*

Below: *Eichmann, in sweater and carpet slippers, writes his memoirs in his Israeli jail cell.*

and Treblinka; Berlin bullies who murdered their enemies in the cellars of the Gestapo HQ on Prinz-Albrechtstrasse.

Wherever they came from and however they killed, they shared equal blame for the suffering they inflicted on mankind during Hitler's twelve years in power.

No physical blood ever stained his hands, but it took a hideously warped mind to plan the systematic murder of millions

It is one thing to be responsible for individual death. Many concentration camp guards and other SS thugs argued at their war crimes trials that they were 'only obeying orders', and that to resist would have meant putting their own necks on the chopping block. Others offered no defence and gloried in their persecution of the defenceless.

THE EVIL MIND OF A MEDIOCRITY

But it took a mind of unfathomable coldness, of deeply twisted logic devoid of human emotions like love and kindness, to pluck the entire, maniacal Holocaust theory out of the Nazis' perverted philosophy and put it into practice. Such a mind belonged to Adolf Eichmann.

Eichmann shares a place in hell with the truly evil criminals who have scorched history. For although his

Right: *Banks of television monitors arrayed for the trial of Eichmann which began on 11 March 1961.*

Below: *Israeli official picture of Eichmann before he was brought into court in Jerusalem before 750 people, mostly members of the world's press.*

uniform was never spattered with an innocent's blood, although he never pulled a trigger in anger, it is accurate to say that he was the biggest mass murderer of them all.

Eichmann made the trains run on time to the infernos of the death camps. He organized the round-ups, the timetables for the 'Final solution to the Jewish Question', and garnered the manpower and hardware necessary to make the whole diabolical scheme possible. At war's end he was the top fugitive Nazi.

Born in 1902 in Solingen, Germany, he grew up in Austria when his father's job as an accountant took him to Linz. Karl Eichmann ran a loveless home which nurtured respect for thrift and order.

As a teenager Adolf did poorly at school and preferred to spend his time daydreaming, talking with the men who had served in the Kaiser's army at the front in World War I, drinking in their tales of glory and sharing their disgust that the politicians, not the soldiers, had lost Germany the war. As Nazism began to thrive in both Germany and Austria he drifted towards the flags and the rhetoric which blamed an international Jewish conspiracy for the defeat.

By the age of twenty Eichmann was employed as a travelling salesman for an oil company. But increasingly he saw his destiny interwoven with the shadow of Hitler's swastika, and on 1 April 1932 he joined the Austrian Nazi party.

THE YOUNG NAZI CONVERT

As the depression throughout Europe and the world worsened in the thirties he left his job to travel to Dachau, twelve miles from Munich, to train at an SS barracks near the infamous concentration camp.

During Eichmann's SS training he had crawled over barbed wire and broken glass - he claimed it made him immune to pain

---

There he was put through gruelling training that left him with permanent scars on his elbows and knees - the legacy of forced crawls over barbed wire and broken glass. 'In that year I rid myself of all susceptibility to pain,' he would later boast. With his training completed Eichmann volunteered for the *Sicherheitsdienst* or SD, the security branch of the SS, and was entrusted in 1935 by its head, Heinrich Himmler, to create a 'Jewish Museum'.

The title was a euphemism for a bureau whose sole task was to collect data on Jewish business and property holdings in Germany and Austria.

Eichmann, the unexemplary student at school, proved himself an astonishingly quick learner when it came to the mortal enemy of the Reich. He plunged into the customs, religion and habits of the Jewish race, quickly establishing himself as an expert in the field.

A TASTE OF POWER

In 1938, with the non-violent annexation of Austria by Germany, came Adolf Eichmann's first taste of absolute power. He was placed in charge of the Office for Jewish Emigration in Vienna.

Using duplicity and brutality in equal measure, he brought terror to the cultured Jewish population of the old imperial capital. Rabbis were dragged from their homes and their heads shaved. Synagogues were razed, businesses looted and homes ransacked.

The victims were stripped of everything they possessed, given a passport bearing the letter 'J' for *Jude* [Jew] and told they had two weeks to find a foreign country to take them in. Failure to do so meant a one-way ticket to a concentration camp.

In Vienna the accountant's son developed a passion for the high life. He lived in the magnificent town house once owned by a member of the Rothschild banking dynasty. He dined at the best restaurants, drank his fill of the splendid vintages arrayed in the Rothschilds' ten thousand-bottle cellar and took a mistress to provide amusement away from his wife of three years.

By 1939 he was under the direct control of Reinhard Heydrich - Hangman Heydrich as he was later known - and was promoted to captain.

Heydrich was charged with selecting hardened SS men for the great tasks which lay ahead in 'cleansing' Europe of her Jews and other undesirables. He saw, after the brilliant success of Eichmann in making Vienna *Judenfrei* or Jew-free,

Below: *Israel was so determined to make a show trial of the Eichmann hearings that they even ran classes for teleprinter operators. The trial's result was a foregone conclusion.*

that he had indeed chosen an admirable sorcerer's apprentice. When he recommended him to Himmler for promotion, Heydrich wrote that Eichmann 'should direct the entire Jewish emigration question'. Eichmann created his own file for it.

He called it the Final Solution.

THE KILLING FACTORIES

When war came later in the year and Poland was over-run, the atrocities began. Poland had an enormous Jewish population and the first extermination centres were set up there.

These were not to be concentration camps. The new centres were factories created for the specific purpose of killing human beings by the hundred thousand.

Under a new department headed by Eichmann called ID IV - but known within the SS ranks simply as the Eichmann Authority - he ordered the construction of ghettoes in major Polish cities like Warsaw and Lodz where the Jews were penned up. He planned for

Above: *Behind bars in an Israeli prison, Eichmann is given a pre-trial medical examination by a police doctor.*

In his office in Berlin Eichmann pressed for more efficient killing methods so that every part of a body - hair, gold teeth, body fat - could be utilized after death. He pushed for the use of Zyklon B gas in the chambers at Auschwitz - colossal rooms masquerading as bathhouses that could 'process' ten thousand human beings every day - and he neatly tabulated the numbers of the dead alongside figures of looted wealth. He also kept count on how many bars of soap were made from the rendered fat of the victims.

THE OBSESSIVE JEW-HUNTER

In 1942, at a villa formerly owned by a prominent Jewish family in the pleasant Berlin suburb of Wannsee, the Nazis made their full and final pact with the devil. Eichmann was there for the conference. There was only one subject on the agenda: 'The final solution of the Jewish question in Europe.'

Right to the end, Eichmann the Nazi zealot remained fiercely proud of what his extermination programme had achieved

---

The Third Reich was embarking on the biggest single crusade of mass murder in history. To uproot Jews from all over Europe, bring them to death factories and kill them without arousing the suspicion of the victims or the neutral countries took masterful planning. Eichmann travelled endlessly throughout Europe, commandeering trains that were needed for the war effort to carry more and more 'enemies of the Reich' to the gas chambers and the ovens.

Not since medieval warlords ruled Europe has such evil power been vested in one man. More pragmatic SS men argued that the extermination of the Jews was secondary to winning the war. Not to Eichmann. He relentlessly continued to press for more freight trucks to transport his victims, more manpower to staff the camps, more gas for the chambers.

In 1944, with the Allies snapping at the gates of Germany, he set off for Hungary where, by dint of the nation's status as a

disease and hunger to take its toll among them so that valuable Reich ammunition would not be wasted.

Eichmann authorized experiments with mobile gas vans - Jews were crammed into sealed trucks and killed by the carbon monoxide gas from the engine exhaust - and he drew up the plans for Auschwitz-Birkenau, in the south, to become the Armageddon for Jews.

Eichmann kept records of how many bars of soap were made from the rendered down fat of concentration camp victims

---

In 1941, when Hitler launched his invasion of the Soviet Union, Eichmann was a lieutenant colonel and the great plains of Russia were to become his personal killing fields for the inferior races. The gas vans had proved themselves to be ineffective and the mass shootings of Jews and Slavs across Russia were time-consuming, costly and traumatic - even for hardened SS men.

German ally, its eight hundred thousand Jews had remained largely free from persecution. Eichmann took this as a personal affront and arrived in Budapest to organize their departure to the death camps. Between mid-May and July 437,000 Jews were sent off on trains to be executed. It was, he said, one of the more gratifying moments in his life.

The unique characteristic of Eichmann was that he believed wholeheartedly in the righteousness of his mission. He saw himself as a subservient disciple of the religion of Nazism who, like a member of a monastic order, deprived himself in his zeal to complete his mission.

By this time the heady grandeur of his earlier times in Vienna, when he had swanned around the city in Rothschild's limousine terrifying hapless rabbis, had evaporated. Instead he was gaunt, tired and thinner - but his eyes burned with the fire of the zealot. He despised those who tried to cover up what had been done in the name of National Socialism.

But the end he refused to see was coming. Allied saturation bombing cut most major rail junctions in Europe, the death camps in Poland had been liberated or destroyed.

In October 1944 he left Budapest on a forced march with hundreds of thousands of civilians as hostages. As he made his way back to a burning, beleaguered Berlin he was able to report to Himmler that, by his reckoning, 4 million Jews had died in the death camps and a further 2 million had been executed by the *Einsatzgruppen* - execution squads - which roamed Russia.

He was a contented man in that so much had been achieved, but concerned that much of his work was left undone. He had, as one historian remarked of him, drenched his soul in blood.

THE HUNTER HUNTED

In the chaos of the final days of the Reich, Eichmann escaped. In April 1945 he made his way with a band of fellow fanatics to the Austrian Tyrol where he hoped to forge a 'Werewolf' unit - a guerrilla group committed to fighting the occupying Allies.

But almost immediately after entering

Below: *Flanked by police in the bullet-proof glass cabin, Adolf Eichmann faces his accusers. On 1 December 1961 he was sentenced to death.*

the mountains his comrades ordered him to leave. His reputation had preceded him and, loyal Germans though they were, they did not want to bc tarred with the same brush. So he wandered down a lonely mountain path with some ammunition and light provisions and set out to lose himself in the chaos engulfing his homeland.

Everywhere there was a price on his head. A ten-man commando unit was formed from death camp survivors in Poland with the specific task of bringing him to justice. With his adjutant, Rudolf Jaenisch, Eichmann made his way through Bavaria wearing the uniform of a Luftwaffe corporal.

Loyal Nazis wanting to fight on after the surrender turned Eichmann away because of his monstrous reputation

---

He was captured twice by American troops. The first time he escaped to Munich, after being put in charge of the holding camp's motor pool, and upon recapture claimed he was a lieutenant in the Waffen [fighting] SS.

At the Oberdachstetten camp in Silesia he led a relatively untroubled existence. But then he heard reports coming through from the war crimes tribunal being assembled in Nuremberg - reports which were laced with the words 'Eichmann', 'monster' and 'mass murder'.

Realizing it was only a matter of time before his true identity was revealed, he set about making plans for a third escape. In January 1946 he got away while working in a road-mending gang. He found his way to the town of Celle where, using the alias Otto Heniger, he lived for four years as a lumberjack.

He knew that he could not stay in Germany: by 1950 the name Eichmann and the extermination of the Jews were inseparable. With the aid of Odessa - the Nazi network of former SS men - he obtained a set of false papers and headed for South America where he vanished, protected by old comrades. Vera Eichmann and their two sons arrived on false papers in Argentina in 1952.

There was no remorse for what had been done during the madness of the Third Reich. He told Dutch Nazi journalist Willem Sassen, in tape-recorded interviews: 'I have to conclude in my own defence that I was neither a murderer nor a mass murderer. I carried out with a clear conscience and faithful heart the duty imposed upon me. I was always a good German, I am today a good German, and I shall always be a good German!'

NEMESIS

In 1957 a blind Jew living in a Buenos Aires suburb, had his curiousity aroused about a man called Ricardo Klement. His daughter had been seeing a young man who called himself Nicholas Eichmann and he stupidly boasted to her that his father's real name was not Ricardo Klement but Adolf Eichmann. It meant nothing to her, but to her old father it meant everything.

Soon the intelligence was in the hands of Isser Harel - founding father of Mossad, the Israeli secret service. Equipped with this scant information he sought permission from David Ben-Gurion, the fledgling state's leader, to mount a mission to bring Eichmann to Israel and to justice.

A hand-picked team of Mossad agents arrived in Buenos Aires in 1958, but the house at 4621 Chacabuco Street was deserted. The Klement family had left there just two months earlier.

It was not until December 1959 that it was picked up again when a Mossad agent discovered that Nicholas Eichmann worked in a motorcycle repair shop in the city. He trailed him to the dismal suburb of San Fernando.

A surveillance team was quickly assembled to stake out the home of Ricardo Klement. For many days the team watched the balding, bespectacled clerk at the local Mercedes Benz plant return home, but they were uncertain it was him.

It wasn't until he appeared on 24 March 1960 clutching a bouquet of flowers that the team were satisfied they had him. A quick check in the Eichmann dossier confirmed that it was his wife's birthday and, like any dutiful husband, he was congratulating her with flowers.

At 8pm on 11 May Adolf Eichmann was snatched by avenging angels of the Mossad. But there was no gratuitous violence on the agents' part. Their prey was bundled into the back seat of a car, covered with a blanket and driven to a safe house.

There his armpit was checked for the tell-tale SS number which every member of the elite had tattooed on him. It was missing, in its place a crude scar.

But there was no pretence on Ricardo Klement's part. He looked calmly at his captors and said in perfect German: '*Ich bin Adolf Eichmann*' - I am Adolf Eichmann.

Ten days later he was aboard an El Al jet bound for Israel. He had been drugged and smuggled out of the country dressed in a pilot's uniform. By the time the aircraft touched down in Israel, Ben-Gurion had already announced to the Knesset that he was under arrest and would be tried in Israel for war crimes.

If the world expected a fanged monster in the dock, it was sadly disappointed. It was only the banality of evil that was exemplified in the bald, shrivelled man in the glass covered stand. He was dressed in a sober suit and looked like a faceless commuter late home from the office.

In his trial, which lasted from 11 April to 14 August 1961, there was no repentance, no hatred, and no bitterness; save that he did not understand why the Jewish people hated him, because he had merely obeyed orders - and surely that was a trait worthy of admiration in any man? Justification for the Holocaust belonged to somebody else.

On 1 December that year he was sentenced to death, and on 31 May 1962 he rejected an appeal by a Protestant minister that he repent as he was led into the death chamber. Refusing a hood as he mounted the scaffold at Ramle Prison, he said: 'Long live Germany. Long live Argentina. Long live Austria. These are the countries with which I have been most closely associated and I shall not forget them. I greet my wife, family and friends. I had to obey the rules of war and my flag. I am ready.'

His remains were cremated and scattered at sea. No prayers of any kind were said for him.

Above: *A neatly suited Eichmann makes a point during his trial, while Judge Moishe Landau wearily rests his face in his hands.*

TED BUNDY
The All-American Killer

'Hi, I'm Ted,' was how a good-looking all-American boy used to introduce himself to women. But he said goodbye in a grotesque ritual of sexual violence - for Theodore Bundy was the worst serial killer the world has ever known

With drop-dead looks and whirlpool eyes, Theodore Bundy was a woman's dream. Three innocent words - 'Hi, I'm Ted' - were his opening lines to his conquests, the blondes, brunettes and redheads who fell under his spell. Handsome, charming, energetic - Bundy attracted women like a magnet pulling paperclips from a box.

But those three little words were also the death sentence for maybe as many as fifty women - for he was the worst - the very worst - serial killer that America and the world have ever known. Using his good looks and charm, he roamed the towns and cities of the USA for four long years like some nomadic angel of death.

His victims died in a sexual frenzy of such intensity that he was alternately labelled the Werewolf, the Vampire and the Ripper slayer. He killed and killed and killed again before he was finally trapped by that most mundane of police methods, the routine check.

His victims died so horribly that Ted Bundy was compared with the werewolves and vampires of horror movies

One of his favourite tricks was a fake plaster cast. He would slip it on, pretend to be lifting a heavy piece of equipment or changing a tyre on his car, and wait for a sympathetic female to offer help. 'Hi, I'm Ted.' The phrase would drip from his lips and the prey was hooked.

Ted Bundy finally 'fried' in Florida's electric chair in 1989, and no tears were shed for him. In fact a local DJ told listeners near the state jail: 'Turn down your coffee makers, folks, because they're gonna need all the juice they can get there today!'

Opposite: *Theodore Bundy in the drab garb of a prisoner - a far cry from the debonair charmer who attracted women like a magnet.*

Below: *Three of Bundy's victims in police files: (from left) Laura Aime, Debbie Kent and Melissa Smith.*

Bundy left behind an astonishing legacy of evil that puts him at the very top of the serial killer tree.

Bundy was a skilful liar, and his psychotic hatred of women began some time during his unhappy childhood. As a teenager he devoured hard-core pornography - which he later blamed for 'triggering the demons' that sent him on the killing spree.

THE BACKGROUND OF A SERIAL KILLER

He was born in a home for unmarried mothers in Burlington, Vermont to nineteen-year-old Louise Cowell, and for the first four years of his life was raised in a modest flat nearby. Later, on the promise of a better job, Louise flew with her son the 3000 miles across America to Seattle. Here she married Johnnie Bundy, a cook at the Madigan Army Hospital on the outskirts of the city. Bundy adopted Ted as his own son, and the couple subsequently had four more children.

Bundy blamed the pornography he had devoured as a teenager for turning him into a violent killer

---

Stamped in the all-American mould, Bundy was a Boy Scout who started the day with a paper round and had a small lawn-mowing business at weekends. He also won a place on the high school track athletics team. His girlfriends then, and later during his years as a law student in Washington, say they were attracted by his looks - but in bed he was sadistic, acting out bondage fantasies.

From high school he entered the University of Puget Sound in Seattle. Later he switched to Washington - where he dropped out in 1967, preferring instead to enrol for a non-degree course in Chinese at Stanford University. His butterfly mind was incapable of studying for long and he dropped out of that course too, heading back west to spend the winter working at odd jobs.

The following year in Seattle he became a volunteer worker for a Republican election campaign before setting off in 1969 to Philadelphia.

Above: *Bundy in his many guises: in 1975 top left; 1976 top right; 1977 middle left and right; 1978 bottom left and right.*

The nationwide flitting is important in the story of Ted Bundy. It gave him a sense of how vast America was and how easy it would be for a criminal to become lost in it.

In a twist of irony, in 1971 he became a counsellor at a rape crisis centre in Seattle. Someone who remembers Bundy from those times is Ann Rule, a real-life sleuth who has chronicled American criminal history in best-selling books.

In the early seventies she worked on the crisis hot-line with Bundy. She says:

When people ask me about Ted I wish I could show them this person that I knew who was everything you would expect a fine, twenty-two-year-old guy would be. He was active in politics, wonderful on the phone, handsome, witty, charming.

I was a friend of Ted Bundy's and I did not expect him to be a serial killer. Never. When I last saw his face before he was executed I saw this same kind of self-deprecating look, the duck of the head, the look that said: 'You can believe this guy.'

Though attracted by his looks, early girlfriends didn't always fall for his sado-masochistic activities in bed

---

Bundy wrote a pamphlet on rape which, with hindsight, was a piece of self analysis: 'A number of rape offenders do not seem to be sick people but individuals who believe they can exert their will over others with impunity.'

THE MURDERS BEGIN

The madness began in 1974 when Ted Bundy was 28 years old.

On 31 January, Lynda Ann Healy, a twenty-one-year-old law student at the University of Washington State, in Seattle, set her alarm for 7am. She had to make a report on skiing conditions for a local radio station and didn't want to be late. Two hours after the designated time the alarm clock was still ringing when her roommate walked in to find her gone, with a one-inch bloodstain on the pillow.

Six weeks later on 12 March Donna Manson walked from her dormitory and headed across the Evergreen State College Campus to a student faculty music recital - and was never seen again.

On 17 April Susan Rancourt, eighteen, left a discussion at the university campus to walk to a cinema 400 yards away. She too vanished as did Roberta Parks, twenty-two, on 6 May, Brenda Ball, twenty-two, on 6 June, and Georgina Hawkins, eighteen, on 16 June.

On 14 July a young man with his arm in a sling was among a crowd of forty thousand sun worshippers lured to the water at Lake Sammamish State Park just

outside Seattle. Janice Orr was sunbathing when he came up to her and said: 'Would you help me put my sailboat on top of my car?' Janice, twenty-three, pushed her bicycle to where his car was. She became victim number seven.

That same afternoon, Denise Naslund went with a group of friends to a sparkling brook that fed into the lake. At 4pm she got out of the water to go to a public lavatory.

Carol DaRonch was called the luckiest teenager in America when she narrowly escaped being victim number twelve

---

Two months later a team of grouse beaters found the remains of both girls scattered under a line of trees. The corpses were stripped of all jewellery and clothes, and they had died in a sexual frenzy of some intensity.

When detectives began investigations they found a number of women who had been approached on that day by a dishy looking man with his arm in a sling. He told them all: 'Hi - I'm Ted.'

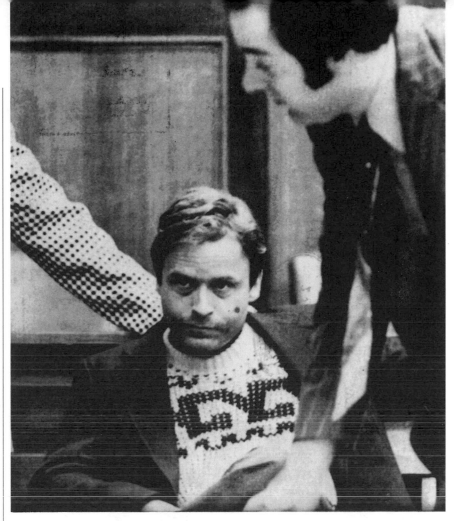

Above: *Ted Bundy sits in court in Pensacola, Florida, before his arraignment. He had twice previously escaped from custody.*

Above: *Bundy chats amiably with the press as he leaves the courthouse at Tallahassee, Florida, where he conducted his own defence against murder charges.*

THE SLAUGHTER SPREADS

On 30 August Bundy left his job at the state's Office of Emergency Services to enrol at the University of Utah law school in Salt Lake City. Two months later the killings had begun in Utah.

Melissa Smith, eighteen - raped and murdered on 18 October. On 31 October - Laura Aime, seventeen, battered and strangled. Debra Kent, also seventeen, died on 8 November. Debra was his second choice that night - Carol DaRonch, eighteen, had a miraculous escape from his VW camper when he handcuffed her after posing as a police officer. Carol managed to roll out of the vehicle as it slowed down in traffic, then fought Bundy on the pavement as he tried to beat her with an iron bar. She was finally rescued by an elderly couple.

The slaughter spread from Utah to Colorado. Bundy claimed the lives of four women between 17 January and April 1975. His blood lust seemed limitless, and to detectives trying to solve the killings - now in three states - Ted Bundy was the worst nightmare: a methodical killer who travelled. With no fixed abode, he could be anyone.

A lucky break for lawmen came in the early hours of 16 August when Utah Highway Patrolman Robert Hayward was sitting in his parked car near his home. With only twenty minutes left on his shift, he was biding his time until 3am when he heard over the radio that two of his deputies were chasing suspected vandals in his town of Granger.

Hayward cranked his vehicle into life and set off to rendezvous with the pursuing officers. But *en route* he saw a VW pull away from the kerbside in front of him, at speed with no lights on. He gave chase to the car.

Although Bundy's VW contained what looked like burglar's or rapist's equipment, he was only booked for a minor traffic offence

---

After twelve blocks Ted Bundy stopped and climbed out to meet Officer Hayward who had drawn his gun. Inside the car the policeman discovered handcuffs, a crowbar, a ski mask and a nylon stocking that Bundy described as 'just some junk'. Amazingly, Bundy was merely booked for failing to stop for a police officer and released on bail.

It wasn't until later, when Utah patrol officers liaised with the murder hunt detectives, that Carol DaRonch's testimony was discovered to match the description of Bundy.

Bundy was arrested the next day in his apartment at 565 First Avenue, Salt Lake City, and charged with possessing tools for burglary. Meanwhile DaRonch identified Bundy from pictures on his driving licence and said the vehicle in

which she had been snatched resembled his. Bundy was out on bail, but the net seemed to be drawing in when two days later, after DaRonch had identified him in a line-up, he was charged with kidnap.

In a further twist, Officer Hayward was the brother of police Captain Bob Hayward, the officer in charge of the DaRonch kidnapping case and the murders of three other women.

A Utah prosecuting attorney later declared that Bundy changed his appearance as often as he did his underpants

---

When Bob spoke to Peter about Bundy a distant alarm bell rang in his brother's mind. In November 1974 a former fiancée of Bundy's, a girl called Liz Kloepfer, had called Peter twice from Seattle, urging him to consider Bundy a suspect in the Utah murders. Hayward

had made routine checks but saw no reason to go any further.

Luck was with Bundy. There was not, at this stage, a shred of solid evidence to tie him into the killings in either state. He was bailed on the charge of a single kidnap and possessing burglary tools.

Women who claimed they had seen him at the lakeside on the day that Orr and Naslund died said they were sure that that man was not Ted Bundy. 'That is because we later found out he changed his appearance ... as often as I changed my shorts,' said Utah prosecutor David Yocum later.

FREE TO KILL AGAIN

Bundy's trial for kidnapping began on 23 February 1976, and he waived his right to a jury trial. He got fifteen years when the trial, after lengthy legal appeals and wrangles, finished in December - but served no time in Utah. Instead he was

Above: *Bundy sits with defence attorney Margaret Good as he hears the jury return a verdict of first-degree murder.*

Above: *Theodore Bundy photographed after his death in the electric chair was finally scheduled. The serial killer's amazing luck had run out.*

Moving quickly upstairs, he entered her room and beat twenty-one-year-old Margaret to death, then strangled her with her own tights before taking great bites out of her buttocks. He moved across the hallway and despatched Lisa Levy, twenty, in the same foul manner.

He beat two others - Karen Chandler and Kathy Kleiner - to the verge of death before fleeing the scene. Both girls were scarred for life and now wear heavy make-up to hide the deep indentations he made on their faces.

On 8 February he killed his youngest-known victim, a ten-year-old girl, Kimberly Leach, in Lake City, Florida, and left her body in a pig-sty.

BUNDY'S LUCK RUNS OUT

The following week luck ran out for Bundy on 15 February when Patrolman David Lee of the Pensacola Police Department became suspicious of a Volkswagen that drove out of a restaurant car park at 3am. A hurried computer check showed that it had been stolen.

> It was for the murder of a little girl of ten that Bundy was finally brought to book

extradited to Colorado to stand trial for the murder of a twenty-year-old student called Carolyn Campbell. On 30 December, using a stack of books and some deft manoeuvring, he escaped through the roof of the Colorado Springs jail, stole a police car and was gone.

On 15 January 1977 came one of his most infamous nights of violence. Armed with a heavy wooden club, he slipped into the Chi Omega sorority house, a female dormitory at the University of Florida in the state capital, Tallahassee. The girls there had just returned from their Christmas holidays.

Diana Cossin had most of the girls in her large room where they sat around swapping gossip into the early hours. Diana, a survivor of that terrible night, said: 'I noticed Margaret Bowman walking past and I said something like: "How are you, Margaret?" And she said: "Life couldn't be better." It was the last time I saw her alive.' When the lights went out, Bundy went in.

After pulling the car over the man identified himself as Ken Misner, attacked the officer and made a run for it. He was tackled, clubbed unconscious, and when he came around told Lee: 'I wish you would have killed me.' Misner was just one of twenty-one identities that Bundy had assumed.

The case against Bundy was assembled painstakingly slowly, but instead of trying to pin dozens of crimes on him he was charged with the single murder of schoolgirl Kimberley. Strong forensic evidence linking him to the killing gave police their best chance of finally nailing him. That evidence came in the form of bite marks that corresponded to his teeth and the marks on her little body.

At his trial Bundy received messages of support, even proposals of marriage, from women who could not believe that so handsome a man could be responsible for such heinous crimes.

He lived in the shadow of the electric

chair for eight years after his conviction for Kimberley's murder and protested his innocence up to the end.

But when Bundy saw there was no way out he broke down and confessed to his grisly catalogue of death - nearly forty murders which, he said, 'I deserve to die for.' Even now police suspect he was still holding out on more crimes.

Sometimes Bundy would fly into a city, then select a victim at random and kill her before flying out again

---

His confession included murders of girls in Idaho, California, Michigan, Pennsylvania and Vermont. Some were committed as 'day trips' when Bundy would jet into a city, select his victim, kill her and then fly out again.

After ten years on death row, he was finally executed at Starke Prison in Florida in February 1989. Religious broadcaster James Dobson spent the final night with Bundy in his cell. Bundy refused his condemned man's last meal, and wept openly as he told Dobson of his perverted crusade of death. Dobson said:

He said society had a right to be protected from him. He said that after he killed the first woman he went through a period of great distress for six months. He was extremely guilty, he didn't believe he could have done something like that. That gradually subsided and that sexual frenzy which he would go through occurred again and he killed another woman to sate it. Each time became a little easier to cope with and he did that so many times that he got to the point where he could not feel any more.

Below: *The body of Ted Bundy is wheeled to the medical examiner's office following his execution at Gainesville, Florida, on 24 January 1989.*

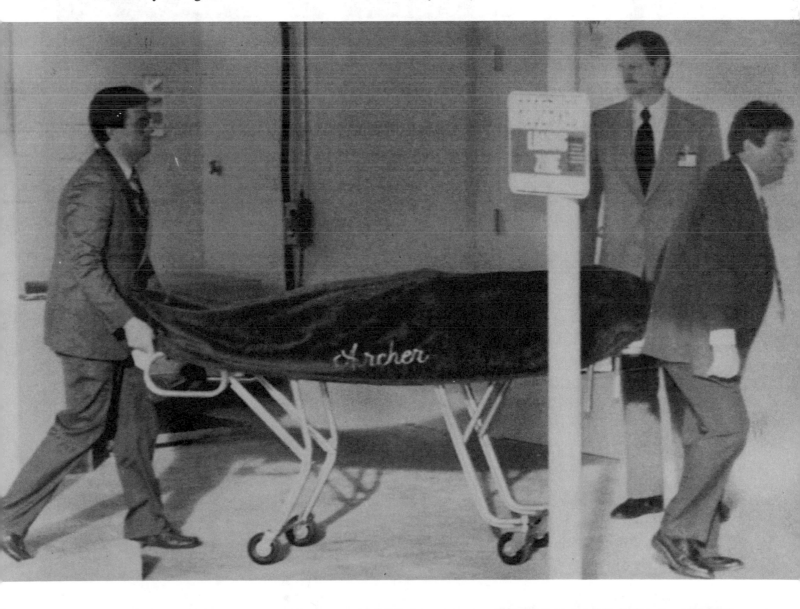

DAVID BERKOWITZ
The Story of Son of Sam

Who was the baby-faced psychotic who stalked the streets of New York in search of innocent young victims? For twelve months 'Son of Sam' held the city in a deadly grip of terror

By day David Berkowitz was a seemingly innocent post office worker, a pudgy, cherubic-faced loner who lived quietly in his tiny suburban apartment.

But by night he was a fiend, the madman whose unearthly alter ego, Son of Sam, would become the most terrifying and mysterious serial killer ever to stalk New York City. For more than twelve months, beginning in July 1976, the curly-haired killer went gunning for attractive victims whose only 'crimes' were their innocence and youth.

Initially dubbed 'the .44-calibre killer' because of the weapon he used in his attacks, Berkowitz killed six of his victims and severely wounded seven others during his reign of terror.

'I love to hunt,' ran Berkowitz's gruesome note. 'Prowling the streets looking for fair game - tasty meat.'

Five of those who died were dark-haired women, sparking a stampede on blonde wigs as frightened women sought to protect themselves. For at the height of the widespread panic the police were helpless to stop the carnage. Moreover, the random nature of the crimes, coupled with the apparent lack of motive, frustrated their efforts - despite the largest manhunt in New York's history.

But what terrified the city almost as much were the bizarre, twisted letters that the twenty-four-year-old Berkowitz sent

to police and to a newspaper columnist at the peak of his rampage. He taunted the city's efforts to track him down, warning that 'I'll be back', and boasting: 'I love to hunt. Prowling the streets looking for fair game - tasty meat.'

A TWISTED MIND

By July 1977 New York was, according to a newspaper account of the time, 'exploding', a city under siege from an unknown terror.

On the surface, the evil that would later be known as Son of Sam began

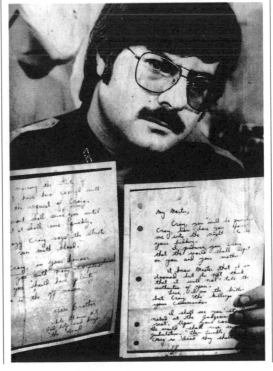

Above: *Police sketches of the killer labelled 'Son of Sam' who brought terror to the streets of New York.*

Opposite: *Drama student Valentina Suriani with her boyfriend Alexander Esau. Both were to fall victim to one of David Berkowitz's murderous frenzies in April 1977.*

Left: *Deputy Sheriff Craig Glassman displays two threatening letters he received from his neighbour Berkowitz. Glassman noticed similarities between his letters and those 'Son of Sam' sent to newspapers.*

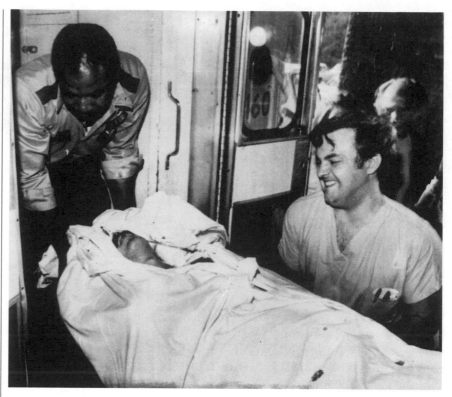

routinely enough in a city where violence is a way of life. Pretty eighteen-year-old Donna Lauria was sitting in a parked car outside her parents' well-kept Bronx apartment with close friend Jody Valente in the early hours of 29 July 1976. Without warning, as Donna opened the car door to leave, a man appeared out of the shadows and stood on the footpath, pulling a .44-calibre gun from a brown paper bag in his left hand.

He crouched, held the gun with both hands and fired three shots, killing the youngster and wounding her friend.

Police were baffled by the senseless killing, but on the streets of New York it was hardly cause for headlines. Within a few days Donna Lauria's name had faded from the newspapers.

THE SERIAL KILLINGS TAKE OFF

For no one could have foreseen that many months later the incident would come back to haunt an entire city.

The unknown assailant would not strike again until 23 October but, luckily for his two helpless victims, this time his aim was off as he fired at a parked car in Flushing, in the borough of Queens.

Carl Denaro, a twenty-year-old who was due to enlist in the US Air Force the

Above left: *Twenty-year-old Stacy Moskowitz, sixth victim of 'Son of Sam', pictured in bed at her Brooklyn home.*

Above: *The critically injured body of Robert Violane after he was attacked by 'Son of Sam' while sitting with his girlfriend Stacy Moskowitz in a Brooklyn lovers' lane.*

following week, was critically wounded by a bullet to the head, but survived. His companion, Rosemary Keenan, eighteen, and the daughter of a police detective, thankfully escaped unhurt.

The overworked New York Police Department failed to notice significant similarities between the first two incidents

---

Again, police ballistic tests showed that the gunman had used a .44-calibre pistol, but it was too early for the alarm bells to ring at Police Headquarters. New York in the 1970s averaged about thirty killings a week, and an overworked police force failed to notice the similarities between the two incidents: the type of gun, the fact that the victims were young and shot while in parked cars, and that the killer struck late at night or early in the morning.

Two more young women were shot and seriously wounded - one was to spend the rest of her life in a wheelchair - when the mysterious gunman surfaced again on 27 November. It wasn't until the faceless force behind the .44 killed his second victim two months later - twenty-six-year-old secretary Christine Freund -

that police finally realized there might be a connection behind the attacks.

The death of Virginia Voskerichian, a Bulgarian-born émigré, in March, made them certain. A madman was on the prowl. Worried city officials immediately organized a .44 Killer Task Force. But even after checking out literally hundreds of leads, police still had neither suspect nor motive.

THE BIRTH OF SON OF SAM

All that changed with the next attack, on 17 April 1977, which left acting student Valentina Suriani and her boyfriend Alexander Esau dead. This time, not only did Berkowitz leave behind two broken bodies cut down in their prime, but also a haunting four-page letter - a missive which gave birth to Son of Sam.

In it, the twisted killer wrote that he was 'deeply hurt' about the descriptions in the press which characterized him as a woman-hater.

I am not. But I am a monster. I am the 'Son of Sam'. I am a little brat. Sam loves to drink blood. 'Go out and kill' commands Father Sam... I am on a different wave length than everybody else - programmed to kill. However, to stop me you must kill me. Attention all police: Shoot me first - shoot to kill or else. Keep out of my way or you will die!

Then, he warned: 'I'll be back! I'll be back!' before signing it, 'Yours in murder, Mr Monster'.

To panic citizens the twisted killer sent one of his sick letters to a newspaper, knowing it would be published

---

The authorities decided against publicizing the letter, though some parts of it were eventually leaked to local newspapers. On 30 May the killer, hoping to heighten the terror, changed his tactics. He wrote directly to Jimmy Breslin, a well-known columnist on the *New York Daily News*. This letter, even

Below: *Berkowitz is taken from Manhattan police headquarters to be charged with the slaying of six young people and the wounding of seven others.*

more nightmarish than the first one, was published in the following day's edition and sent the city into the fearful panic Son of Sam had craved.

It began:

Hello from the gutters of NYC, which are filled with dog manure, vomit, stale wine, urine and blood. Hello from the sewers of NYC which swallow up these delicacies when they are washed away by the sweeper trucks. Hello from the cracks in the sidewalks of NYC and from the ants that dwell in these cracks and feed on the dried blood of the dead that has seeped into these cracks.

The killer cautioned Breslin not to think he had finished his 'work'.

Mr Breslin, sir, don't think that because you haven't heard from [me] for a while that I went to sleep. No, rather, I am still here. Like a spirit roaming the night. Thirsty, hungry, seldom stopping to rest; anxious to please Sam... I love my work... Sam's a thirsty lad and he won't let me stop killing until he gets his fill of blood.

On the back of the envelope was written:

Blood and Family,
Darkness and Death,
Absolute Depravity,
.44

It was as though Son of Sam was writing from the very depths of hell.

On 25 June the gunman struck again, seriously wounding a young woman and her date in a parked car in Queens.

New York was in panic, and as the police seemed powerless, vigilante groups sprang up. In one incident a Brooklyn burglar was caught carrying a large-calibre gun, and a mob slung a noose from a lamp-post ready to lynch him. It took a dozen policemen to free the man from his irate captors.

In the days after the attack, from the seedy bars of the Bronx to the élite business clubs of Manhattan a terrified populace turned its attention to the calendar. Would Son of Sam 'celebrate' the black anniversary of his first attack on 29 July 1976?

Since the police seemed powerless, trigger-happy vigilante groups sprang up all over the terrified city

---

Berkowitz may have been a brute but he was not a fool. He was well aware that every available policeman throughout the metropolitan area would be on the lookout that night. So he let the date pass without incident - but his lust for blood couldn't be suppressed for long.

In fact he chose the very next night to commemorate his evil, killing Stacy Moskowitz and critically injuring her date, Robert Violante, as they sat in a parked car in Brooklyn.

New York exploded in fear and violence, as more vigilante gangs began attacking people they believed were the elusive Son of Sam. And yet the days of Berkowitz's reign of terror were fast coming to a close - thanks to a stroke of good fortune and a bizarre coincidence.

WHO WAS DAVID BERKOWITZ?

But just who was this unknown madman who, just days later, would be making the front page coast to coast? He was born illegitimate in Brooklyn, New York, on 1 June 1953, and raised by adoptive parents Nathan and Pearl Berkowitz. They were a hard-working, blue-collar couple who saw to it that David led as

Below: A bearded Berkowitz calls a press conference at Attica prison, New York State, minutes before a judge refused to rule him competent to handle his own defence.

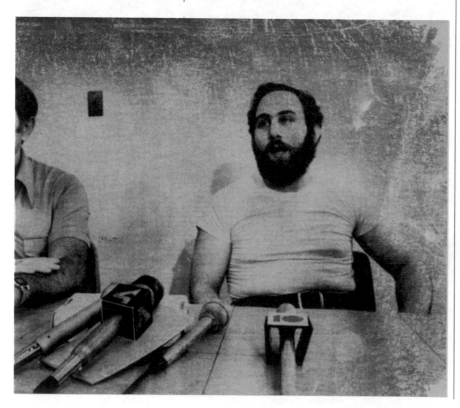

fundamentalist Christianity. Indeed, so complete was the change that Berkowitz often tried to convert fellow soldiers and residents of Louisville, Kentucky where he was stationed for a time.

***

While he was in the Army Berkowitz got hooked on fundamentalist Christianity

***

On his return to New York, in the late spring of 1974 Berkowitz was hired as a security guard and moved into a small apartment in his native Bronx. It was shortly after his return to civilian life that the events began to unfold which would eventually help turn the tubby, religious Berkowitz into the madness of Son of Sam. First his father, from whom he had been estranged for some time, left New York for retirement in Florida. Next, in his search to find his real mother he discovered that he was illegitimate.

These events left Berkowitz a brooding drifter. By February 1976, five months before he began the slaughter, he moved from his Bronx home to nearby New Rochelle. But after two months, he abruptly changed addresses, to Yonkers, 25 miles north of the city. Eventually he joined the US Postal Service.

THE FATAL MISTAKE

He was still sorting mail ten days after the Moskowitz murder, when the police department in Yonkers received a call from a Detective James Justus at the 10th Precinct in Brooklyn.

Justus, a veteran member of the NYPD, had been telephoning owners of cars which had been given parking tickets near the Moskowitz death scene. It was a boring, routine part of police work, but Justus was an experienced cop, and knew it had to be done.

His repeated telephone calls to the owner of a 1970 four-door Galaxie, cream-coloured with a black vinyl roof - which had been ticketed just thirty minutes before the most recent murder - went unanswered. So he decided to ask the Yonkers police force to notify the man, one David Berkowitz, and ask him to call the 10th Precinct.

normal a childhood as possible. He was of above-average intelligence at school, popular with his classmates and baseball team-mates - though acquaintances would later reveal that his love life was virtually non-existent.

But when he was fourteen, his adoptive mother succumbed to cancer, a tragedy from which the troubled teenager would never fully recover.

By the time he was eighteen, David, who had long liked uniforms, decided to join the Army, much to the chagrin of his recently remarried father. But Berkowitz was insistent, and in June 1971 enlisted. He stayed in the Army, for three years.

His service was unremarkable, except for a few minor disciplinary charges and his apparent conversion from Judaism to

Above: A posed prison photograph of 'Son of Sam' David Berkowitz.

Inset: A note found by police in Berkowitz's car when they arrested him outside his apartment in Yonkers, New York, in October 1977.

Above: *A police officer displays a .44-calibre Charter Arms Bulldog revolver, found fully loaded in Berkowitz's apartment.*

Justus spoke to switchboard operator Wheat Carr - an incredible coincidence given her family's association with Berkowitz which later came to light - and explained the problem. When he mentioned Berkowitz's name, Justus was amazed at her response.

'He is the guy that I think is responsible,' she told him. Carr went on to describe bizarre incidents involving Berkowitz, including claims that he had shot her dog with a .44-calibre gun and had been sending threatening notes to her father, whose name was - Sam.

A casual conversation with a switchboard operator gave Detective Justus astounding information about the killer's identity

---

Justus immediately reported all this to his superiors. And yet they weren't particularly excited because they had been receiving worthless tips about thousands of suspected 'Sons of Sam'. Still, they realized Berkowitz had to be interviewed. So the following day Detectives Ed Zigo and John Longo were sent up to Yonkers.

After locating his apartment building on Pine Street they spotted his vehicle parked about thirty yards down the quiet street. They went over to investigate.

Through the window they noticed a rifle butt protruding from a duffel bag. They decided to probe more fully.

In the glove box was an envelope addressed to Timothy Dowd, a deputy inspector who was leading the task force. Zigo opened it and read the enclosed letter, which Berkowitz had intended leaving at the side of his next victim.

It promised more attacks - including a planned massacre at a posh nightclub on the eastern tip of Long Island. The police had found their Son of Sam.

Fifteen police gun barrels were aimed at him, but Berkowitz merely smiled and said, 'What took you so long?'

Zigo called for back-up units while legal experts began organizing a warrant to search the apartment. But there was no need for such formalities that night, because just before 10pm, the night stalker himself, dressed in jeans, brown boots and a short-sleeved white shirt, appeared out of the doorway of the building. He was carrying a brown paper bag, which the police would discover contained a .44-calibre gun.

Not realizing that his days as Son of Sam were about to end Berkowitz sauntered casually to his car, so confident in his own evil power that he didn't even bother to look around. He got in, turned the ignition...and looked up to see the barrels of fifteen guns levelled at him.

'Police! Don't move!' the officers screamed.

Berkowitz smiled that eerie smile. 'Okay,' he said softly. 'You've got me. What took you so long?'

ARREST OF A SATANIST

Those present at the scene would later recall how he met his fate with icy detachment. Following the arrest, Berkowitz was ferried back to Manhattan police headquarters.

Word of Son of Sam's capture had already been leaked to the media, and they were on the scene at One Police Plaza when the convoy arrived. But instead of seeing a chained, wild-eyed beast they saw David Berkowitz, smiling and looking as dangerous as a lamb.

Nevertheless, behind that vacuous smile lurked a madman. Six hours after his arrest, the interrogation began...and even veteran law enforcement authorities were stunned by the twisted mind that sat before them. Sam, Berkowitz told them, was the person responsible for the crimes because he kept ordering them.

'Who is Sam?' asked Ronald Aiello, head of the homicide bureau at the Brooklyn District Attorney's office.

'My master.' In fact, the police later discovered, the killer was referring to his neighbour Sam Carr - whose barking dog had bothered him.

'Do you want to tell me how you got those orders?'

'Yes, he told me through his dog, as he usually does. It's not really a dog. It just looks like a dog. It's not. He just gave me an idea where to go. When I got the word, I didn't know who I would go out to kill - but I would know when I saw the right people.'

Berkowitz was grilled for almost two hours, confessing to all the crimes.

During his stay at the Kings County Hospital for psychiatric evaluation, Berkowitz answered a letter smuggled in from Steve Dunleavy, a columnist on the *New York Post*. His reply spoke of Sam as 'one of the devils of Satan...a force beyond the wildest imaginations of people. He is not human.'

'When I killed,' he ranted, 'I really saved many lives... People want my blood but they don't want to listen to what I have to say. There are other Sons out there - God help the world.'

According to one psychiatrist, killing a woman was the only way that Berkowitz could achieve sexual gratification

---

It was in part the declaration that 'other' depraved killers like him were loose in the world that has led some private investigators, writers and even law enforcement officials to suspect that Berkowitz had not acted alone, that he was part of some demonic cult.

Still, at his subsequent trial he admitted all guilt, and the only psychiatrist to judge Berkowitz sane after his arrest, Dr David Abrahamsen, says Son of Sam was driven to kill by a deep fear of women, not by Satanic influences.

'He could not approach a woman as a man would do and have sex with her or date,' Abrahamsen told an interviewer. 'That was not for him. I think he developed a great deal of contempt for women. He's very, very dangerous.'

Below: *Four victims of the 'Son of Sam' killer: (from left) Valentina Suriani, Christine Freund, Virginia Voskerichian and Stacy Moskowitz.*

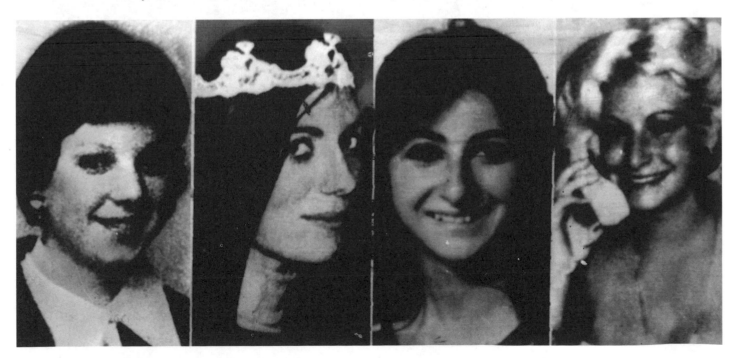

CHARLES MANSON
Hollywood Murderer

Even in the drug-crazed, hippie seventies this was a mass murder that shook America. The perverted, maniacal cult leader Charles Manson and his disciples were responsible for two days of evil that went beyond society's worst nightmares

I n August 1970, on an old movie ranch not far from the sprawling, sun-baked city of Los Angeles, a motley group of hippie drop-outs, bikers and petty criminals sat amid the ramshackle, decaying buildings listening to the eerie words of a small, bearded man whom many of them considered a prophet.

It was time, he quietly told them, for Helter Skelter, the beginning of his visionary race war between black and white that would cleanse the earth for all time and pave the way for his reign as master of an entire planet.

With that macabre declaration Charles Manson, pimp, thief and failed musician, unleashed on the world a terror that even today continues to haunt and horrify.

AN ORGY OF BLOOD-LETTING

By the time the twisted, two-day orgy of blood-letting was over, seven people, including the beautiful young actress Sharon Tate, who was more than eight months pregnant with her first child, had been savagely butchered - their blood used to scrawl bizarre, taunting messages on the walls and doors of their homes.

No money had been stolen, despite the obvious wealth of all the victims. And there was no revenge motive - only the senseless slaughter of seven human beings whose sole 'crime' had apparently been that they were successful. The crimes would become known around the world as the Tate-LaBianca murders.

For several weeks investigators came up empty-handed despite checking thousands of leads and tips. The bizarre discovery was to come only after five painstaking months of futile search.

Above: *An early picture of Charles Manson with his beard shaved and hair cut.*

Left: *Scruffy, bearded Manson walks to the Los Angeles court room where he is to stand trial for the murder of Sharon Tate and six others.*

Opposite: *Gloating, mad Manson, his beard now greying, wears a swastika on his forehead as he faces a parole board in San Quentin prison.*

Above: *Sharon Tate, butchered at her Benedict Canyon home on the night of 9 August 1969, along with four others.*

Above right: *Scene of slaughter in the living room of Sharon Tate's home in Los Angeles. Bodies were found in front of the couch and outside the house.*

The big break came quite by accident. The police arrested a suspect in another, seemingly unrelated, murder.

Susan Atkins, a veteran of countless acid trips whose flower child innocence masked what even Manson described as 'the most perverted imagination' in the so-called Family, was picked up in connection with the murder of drug dealer Gary Hinman ten days before Tate and the others were massacred.

It was as if Manson had let loose a pack of demons from hell into the heart of Hollywood

---

While awaiting arraignment, Atkins began to brag to fellow inmates about her role in the Tate-LaBianca murders. She claimed she had even tasted the pregnant actress's blood, and spoke reverently of the 'Family' leader - a living god who had the power to make his followers do anything he wished.

Atkins was gloating as her tale of terror unfolded, especially when it came to the death of the actress herself.

'It felt so good the first time I stabbed her, and when she screamed at me it did something to me...and I stabbed her again. I just kept stabbing her until she stopped screaming. It was like a sexual release. Especially when you see the blood. It's better than a climax.'

Two of those privy to the disclosures tipped off the police who, by a stroke of pure coincidence, had already rounded up the cult members charging them with unrelated arson and car theft charges.

'It was like a sexual release. Especially when you see the blood. It's better than a climax,' boasted Susan Atkins

---

Days later, in a bid to play down her role in the killings, Atkins told her tale to the *Los Angeles Times*, deliberately omitting her previous confession. Within hours the story had been flashed around the world - and Manson was the most talked about criminal in the annals of American law enforcement.

ORIGINS OF A CULT LEADER

Charles Manson was born the illegitimate son of a cold, uncaring prostitute in Cincinnati, Ohio in 1935. The young Charlie, who never knew his real father,

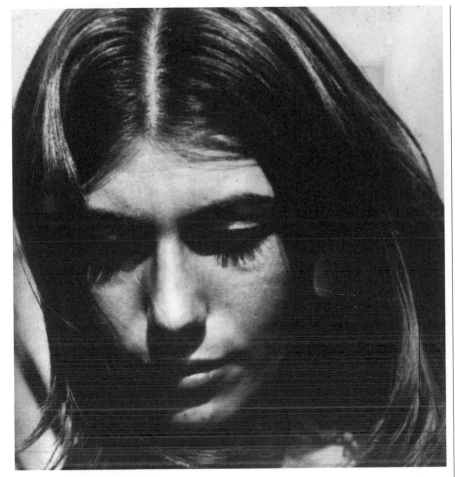

spent his most formative years bouncing between several foster homes.

The rebellious youngster had little inclination for school, and his transition from child to teenager was marked by petty criminal enterprises and stints in various corrective institutions.

On 9 March 1951 he was sentenced to the National Training School for Boys in Washington, DC. But just before he was due for a parole hearing, in February the following year, he held a razor blade to another boy's throat while he raped him. This incident got him transferred to the Federal Reformatory in Virginia. He remained there until May 1954.

Even though his sexual experiences had until this point been homosexually oriented, shortly after his parole he met a seventeen-year-old waitress, Rosalie Jean Willis, and married her. He and his pregnant bride travelled to California, but Manson could never reform - he stole the car they used for the trip, and was sentenced to three years' jail.

He was still incarcerated when Charles Manson Jr was born. Rosalie made

Above: Susan Atkins, one of Manson's 'love slaves', who faced trial alongside her evil Svengali. She said of Sharon Tate: 'It felt so good the first time I stabbed her.'

frequent visits, but in 1957 the visits stopped - Rosalie had found real love with another man.

Manson was paroled the following year, but continued to be constantly in trouble with the law. In between his many prison terms he found time to remarry and sire a second son.

Just before his parole hearing, seventeen-year-old Manson held a razor blade to another boy's throat while he raped him

---

It was now 1964, and Manson, like many young Americans, became infatuated with the Beatles. But unlike the millions of other fans of the Fab Four, Charlie's obsession with the band turned into fanaticism.

In 1967, Manson, now thirty-two, was finally released. He asked the authorities if he could stay in jail. But they refused, so he drifted to San Francisco. Here he fell in with the simple flower children of Haight-Ashbury. Armed with little more than a guitar and the clothes on his back, Manson had finally found his niche - a wolf among lambs.

AMONG THE DROP-OUTS

The shaggy folk singer with a street-wise philosophy was an instant hit with the drop-outs and drug addicts of the area, a messianic Pied Piper. He, in turn, found something he had always craved - a sense of belonging and an attentive, easily manipulated audience.

By 1969 Manson and his followers, mainly adoring young women who had abandoned their middle-class roots, drifted south. Eventually they moved to the old Spahn Ranch outside Los Angeles, where they established the beginnings of 'The Family'. Soon afterwards other disillusioned youngsters were joining the ragtag group.

Together they would smoke marijuana, drop acid and dance naked under the stars of the Californian desert, all the while eagerly listening to Charlie's ramblings - a complex fusion of the Beatles, the Bible and his own twisted bitterness towards the society that had spurned him.

Charlie, as witnesses would later recount, announced it was time for Helter Skelter. Soon the race war would begin. According to his twisted mind the blacks would emerge victorious, destroying the white race forever - everyone, that is, except for him and his motley band.

Manson and his disciples would take drugs and dance naked together at their commune in the Californian desert

---

Then, he asserted, the blacks would turn to the Family - which by this time would have grown to 144,000 (Charlie's 'Chosen People', which he got from the biblical reference to the twelve tribes of Israel, each numbering twelve thousand).

Manson had grandiose dreams and believed he would come to rule the entire planet. According to Greg Jakobson, a talent scout who knew him, Manson also believed 'the Beatles were spokesmen'.

'They were speaking to Charlie, through their songs, letting him know from across the ocean that this is what was going to go down,' said Jakobson.

It was the bizarre 'Revolution 9' that Manson spoke of most. 'It was the Beatles' way of telling people what was going to happen,' said Jakobson ... 'it directly paralleled the Bible's Revelation 9.' The biblical reference was to the battle of Armageddon, and in Charlie's mind, it was a call to the black man that it was time for Helter Skelter. But the blacks, he believed, needed 'help' in

Above: Victims of the Manson cult raid: (from left) Voytek Frykowski, Sharon Tate, Steven Parent, Jay Sebring and Abigail Folger.

Below: Manson leaves the court after asking to be allowed to conduct his own defence.

starting the race war. That's where he and the Family would fit in. They would strike at the heart of the white Establishment, leaving behind 'clues' that indicated a murderous rampage by a gang of radical blacks. Helter Skelter would get a kick start.

THE HORROR OF HELTER SKELTER

And so, in the pre-dawn hours of 9 August 1969, Manson despatched four black-clad Family members, three of whom were women: Susan 'Sadie' Atkins, a former church choir singer; Patricia Krenwinkel, a one-time office secretary; and Linda Kasabian, who would later prove instrumental in the prosecution's case. The lone male was

Charles 'Tex' Watson, who had been a star athlete back in his Texan high school.

Together the four 'Angels of Death' drove into the prestigious Benedict Canyon section of Los Angeles and made a brief stop on top of a hill with a view of 10050 Cielo Drive, the mansion which Sharon Tate and her film director husband Roman Polanski were renting. There, Watson cut the telephone wires, before proceeding to the estate.

They scaled the fence and crept down the drive to the house. They crept inside and the slaughter began.

Tate, just twenty-six, was later found butchered along with three friends and a caretaker's guest. She had been stabbed sixteen times. Her foetus, a boy due any day, died along with her.

The other victims were similarly massacred. As Watson clubbed and stabbed Voytek Frykowski, a Polish film director, he whispered: 'I am the devil, come to do the devil's work.' Steven Parent, the eighteen-year-old guest of the caretaker, was stabbed four times; Jay Sebring, Hollywood's premier hair stylist, was shot and stabbed. Abigail Folger, a coffee heiress, was stabbed on the front lawn as she tried to flee.

'I am the devil, come to do the devil's work,' whispered 'Tex' Watson as he clubbed and stabbed one victim to death

---

Before the marauders left, they used the blood of their victims to scrawl 'Pig' on the front door of the mansion.

But even as Los Angeles reeled in shock, Manson was planning his next murderous move. This time he himself would lead the attacks.

The very next night, he and three disciples broke into the home of Leno and Rosemary LaBianca, owners of a small supermarket chain. He personally tied the victims up, then left them to await a slow, agonizing death at the hands of his devil children - Watson, Krenwinkel and pretty Leslie Van Houten, a former college beauty queen.

According to the gruesome testimony which would come out at the trial months later, the three maniacs carved away at their helpless victims with knives and forks they had found in the kitchen. Krenwinkel carved the word 'war' in the stomach of the dead Leno LaBianca, and left a fork protruding from his stomach.

At first the police did not link these killings to the Tate murders. Quantities of cocaine and marijuana had been found in and around the Polanski mansion, and the authorities had speculated that the murders could have been the result of a drug deal gone horribly wrong.

Yet the police's single-minded belief in the drug motive made them ignore a vital clue. Soon after the slaughter on Cielo Drive two detectives working on another murder case, that of Gary Hinman, told their superiors that at the death scene, just as had occurred in the Tate killings, the murderers had scrawled on the wall a message, 'political piggy', using the victim's own blood. They further explained that they had arrested a

Below: *Manson arrives at the Los Angeles court - wearing a purple velvet shirt and gold corduroy trousers.*

suspect, Bobby Beausoleil, who was part of a bizarre hippie clan in the desert headed by a guy named Charlie.

But the officials refused to believe there was a connection. It wasn't until Atkins began confiding in her cellmates that the truth became known.

A MADMAN ON TRIAL

When the real culprits were finally caught, Manson's tribe of slavishly devoted followers added a new dimension to an already bizarre case.

The rich and famous, it became known, had been slaughtered by children of privilege, who had left their comfortable middle-class homes for a life of drugs, sex and murder.

At the nine-month-long trial, it was Manson himself who addressed the underlying fear that his disciples had engendered. In a rambling one-hour statement, he sounded almost eloquent.

'These children who come at you with knives, they're your children,' he began.

I didn't teach them. You did. I just tried to help them stand up...Most of the people at the ranch that you call the Family were just people that you did not want...So I did the best I could and I took them up on my garbage dump and I told them this: that in love there is no wrong.

Above: *Shaven-headed Manson in the early days of his prison sentence.*

Below: *Manson is led away from court after being found guilty of first-degree murder on all seven counts.*

...I am only what lives inside each and every one of you...

I never went to school, so I never growed up to read and write so good, so I have stayed in jail and I have stayed stupid and I have stayed a child while I watched your world grow up, and then I look at the things that you do and I don't understand.

But then, as his eyes widened and his voice boomed, courtroom observers saw a glimpse of the madness, and the mesmerizing power over others, that was Manson:

Fascinated courtroom spectators observed how Manson's mesmerizing power would make others do his bidding unquestioningly

---

If I could, I would jerk this microphone off and beat your brains out with it, because that's what you deserve, that's what you deserve...Is it a conspiracy that the music is telling the youth to rise up against the Establishment?...The music speaks to you every day, but you are too deaf, dumb and blind to even listen to the music...There are many, many more, coming in the same direction. They are running in the streets - and they are coming right at you!

Indeed, during the trial Manson's words appeared to be coming true. He was considered a heroic martyr by many disillusioned teens and counter-culture revolutionaries, and the underground press praised him as an 'innocent man' fighting the oppressive establishment.

SOCIETY'S VERDICT

On Monday, 29 March 1971, after what was then the longest criminal trial in American history, the jury returned guilty verdicts on all counts against Manson and his robotic disciples of death.

Three weeks later, Judge Charles Older sentenced the defendants to death. But the sentences were commuted to life imprisonment in 1972, when California's death penalty was outlawed.

Today Charlie is just as frightening as ever. At fifty-six he still gets stacks of mail from troubled youngsters. He spends his days strumming his guitar or making model scorpions out of whatever is available in his solitary confinement at a maximum-security prison in California.

He has even written about himself in a book called *Manson, In His Own Words*, co-authored by a former prison cell mate and published in 1988.

As for the followers who carried out the killings to 'fulfil' his prophecy, all of them are still in prison. However, unlike Charlie, they appear to have changed their demonic ways. Susan Atkins, now

forty-three, is a married, born-again Christian. Leslie Van Houten, forty, has obtained a college degree in literature and psychology.

The third woman convicted for the murders is Patricia Krenwinkel, now forty-three. In November 1989 her parole appeal was denied.

'I want you to know that I've got everything in the world,' Manson wrote from jail in 1988. 'At my will, I walk your streets, and am there among you'

'Tex' Watson, now a forty-six-year-old born-again Christian, is serving his life sentence in the California Men's Colony in San Luis Obispo. He has become a member of the prison chaplain's staff. He is married, and has three children.

Linda Kasabian, who was the star witness at the trial and was granted immunity from prosecution, is now forty-two. She lives in rural New Hampshire, raising her four children.

Manson himself professes not to care about his slim prospects of ever walking free: 'I want you to know,' he wrote from his jail cell in 1988, 'that I've got everything in the world, and beyond, right here. At my will, I walk your streets, and am out there among you.'

Left: *Susan Atkins arriving in court for the hearing wearing a long cotton dress.*

Below: *Charles Manson, by now showing every sign of madness, during a prison interview with a reporter at San Quentin.*

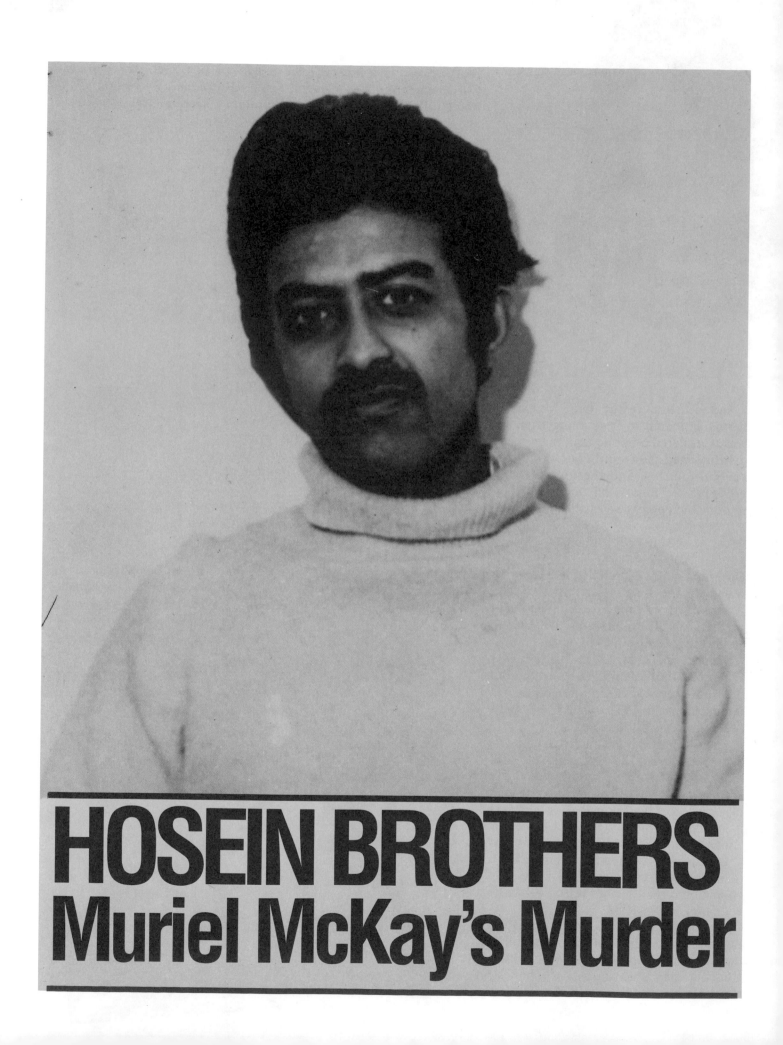

HOSEIN BROTHERS
Muriel McKay's Murder

A middle-aged suburban housewife is kidnapped - and for her newspaper husband the tabloid headlines of his working day become a dreadful nightmare reality. But to this day only her kidnappers know what grisly fate really befell Muriel McKay

The world of Muriel McKay was one of genteel, suburban luxury, far removed from the cut-and-thrust life of her husband Alick. As number two to newspaper tycoon Rupert Murdoch and deputy chairman of the mass circulation *News of the World*, he was in daily contact with stories of crime and vice.

Mrs McKay, however, saw her husband off to work in the morning and was happy to spend her day looking after their expensive home in Wimbledon, South London, a stone's throw away from the All England tennis club.

It was a cosy, comfortable world for the forty-eight-year-old housewife... a world that on the night of 29 December 1969 she was to leave for ever.

KIDNAP IN SUBURBIA

Alick McKay returned home to St Mary House in the tree-lined Arthur Road at 8pm and knew immediately that something was wrong. The front door was unlocked, which worried him since he and Muriel had taken the utmost care after a burglary some months before.

As he stepped through the door he saw a tin of sticking plaster, a ball of string and a meat cleaver

As he stepped into the hall, he found his wife's handbag open on the floor, its contents strewn on the staircase. On a table was a tin of plasters, a ball of thick string and a menacing-looking meat

Above: *The genteel, suburban home from which Mrs Muriel McKay was abducted on the evening of 29 December 1969.*

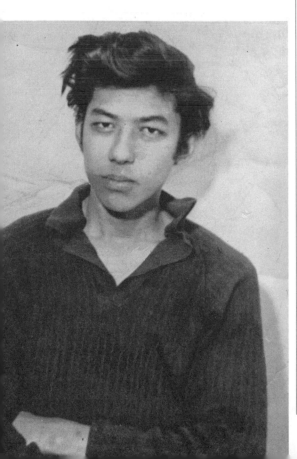

Opposite: *Arthur Hosein was nicknamed by villagers 'King Hosein' because of his boasts that he would one day become a millionaire.*

Left: *Nizamodeen Hosein who, with his brother, trailed Rupert Murdoch's Rolls Royce - to the wrong house.*

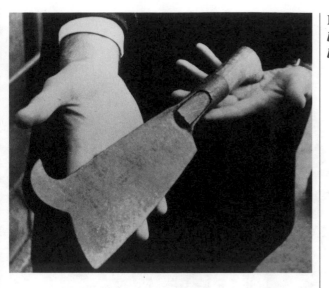

Left: *A meat cleaver found by police at the Hosein brothers' farmhouse.*

cleaver. Alick yelled out his wife's name, grabbed the cleaver and dashed upstairs. There was no sign of Muriel. The distraught husband raced to a neighbour's house and called the police.

Hours later, as the officers swarmed over the house taking fingerprints, Alick received a phone call.

Caller: *This is Mafia Group Three. We are from America, Mafia M Three. We have your wife.*

Alick: *You have my wife?*

Caller: *You will need a million pounds by Wednesday.*

Alick: *What are you talking about? I don't understand.*

Caller: *Mafia. Do you understand?*

Alick: *Yes, I have heard of them.*

Caller: *We have your wife. It will cost you one million pounds.*

'Please co-operate', ran the anguished message, 'for I cannot keep going ... What have I done to deserve this?'

Alick: *This is ridiculous. I haven't anything like a million.*

Caller: *You had better get it. You have friends. Get it from them. We tried to get Rupert Murdoch's wife. We couldn't get her, so we took yours instead.*

Alick: *Rupert Murdoch?*

Caller: *You have a million by Wednesday or we will kill her. Understand?*

Alick: *What do I do?*

Caller: *All you have to do is wait for the contact. You will get the instructions.*

Have the money or you won't have a wife. We will contact you again.

The line went dead and police were unable to trace the call.

At 8 the next morning the postman arrived with a letter. Inside, on a piece of cheap blue paper was a message in Muriel's handwriting.

It read: *Please do something to get me home. I am blindfolded and cold. Please co-operate for I cannot keep going. I think of you constantly and the family and friends. What have I done to deserve this treatment? Love, Muriel.*

A CLAIRVOYANT IGNORED

Over the next few days Alick heard nothing more from his wife or her kidnappers. But a Dutch clairvoyant,

Below: *'Have you seen this woman?' The poster that went up around Britain after Mrs McKay's disappearance.*

METROPOLITAN POLICE
HAVE YOU SEEN THIS WOMAN?

Missing from her home at Wimbledon since evening of 29th December, 1969.

Height 5ft. 9in., medium build, dark brown hair, brownish green eyes, dark complexion, Australian accent.

Wearing black cashmere reversible coat, fawn coloured wool on reverse side, no button. Green jersey suit.   Cream patent shoes, square toes, 1¼in. heel, yellow metal chain across instep.

IF YOU HAVE SEEN Mrs. McKay since 5 p.m. on 29th December, 1969, please inform Wimbledon Police Station at 01-946 1113, or your nearest Police Station.

Printed by the Receiver for the Metropolitan Police District, New Scotland Yard, S.W.1

Gerard Croiset, who had accurately pinpointed the graves of the child victims in the Moors Murders case, claimed that Muriel was being held on the borders of Essex and Hertfordshire, some forty miles north of London. Police ignored his guidance - to their cost.

It was not until 20 January that the thirty-strong team of detectives assigned to the case got their first breakthrough. It was another letter from Muriel, posted in Wood Green, north London:

I am deteriorating in health and spirit. Please co-operate. Excuse handwriting, I am blindfolded and cold. Please keep the police out of this and co-operate with the gang giving Code M3 when telephoning you. The earlier you get the money, the quicker I may get home or you will not see me again. Darling can you act quickly? Please, please keep the police out of this if you want to see me. Muriel.

The villagers of Stocking Pelham called West Indian tailor Arthur 'King Hosein' because of his grandiose ideas

---

The following day there were three phone calls from the kidnappers issuing instructions on where to leave the ransom money. Alick demanded proof that his wife was still alive; the gang sent a package containing three pieces of material from Muriel's green wool outfit and a snip of leather from her shoes.

From a stamp on the package, forensic experts managed to get one thumbprint. It was later a crucial piece of evidence.

The ransom was to be handed over in two payments of £500,000. Alick gave police £300 in used notes, but the rest of the 'money' would consist of cut-up newspapers. There were two or three attempts at a handover, but they failed.

Finally, Friday, February 5 was the date demanded by Muriel's captors. The cash was to be dropped near Bishop's Stortford in Hertfordshire. Police staked out the area. But no one picked up the bait. The waiting officers, however, did spot a Volvo saloon cruising the area. The registration number ' XGO 994G ' had been noted at an earlier failed handover attempt. A check revealed the car belonged to a man called Arthur Hosein.

He was a West-Indian born tailor who aspired to be accepted in English middle-class society.

In 1967 he and his German wife Else had bought Rooks Farm in the village of Stocking Pelham, just a few miles from Bishop's Stortford. And within months Arthur's younger brother Nizamodeen had moved in with them. Villagers called

Above: *Mrs Elsa Hosein, German-born wife of Arthur, on her way to the Old Bailey to see her husband stand trial.*

day dawned on 6 February, twenty detectives swooped on Rooks Farm. When Else answered the door they told her that they were investigating a cache of stolen jewellery.

The police were impressed by Arthur's calm manner. 'I earn a lot of money,' he told them. 'I do not deal in stolen goods. You may search where you like.'

But when they began the search they soon knew they were on the right track. First an officer emerged from a bedroom with scraps of blue notepaper identical to the kind used in the ransom notes.

Then they discovered a writing pad on which could be made out the indentation of words written in Muriel's handwriting. The officers also unearthed a sawn-off shotgun which had recently been fired.

Was Muriel McKay's dismembered body put into the pigswill at Rooks Farm?

What they did not find was any trace of Mrs McKay herself - alive or dead.

But there was one discovery that morning which was to lead to the most gruesome theory. Traces of bone were found in a fireplace, and a billhook which had been used to slaughter animals.

Arthur Hosein said he had borrowed it from a farmer to 'cut up a calf'. He added, chillingly: 'We fed it to the dogs and put the bones and head in with the rubbish which we fed to the pigs.'

The brothers had recently sold several pigs but police were unable to trace them. If they had been, they might have confirmed their theory: that Muriel McKay had been murdered and her dismembered body put into the pigswill.

CHARGED WITH MURDER

In any event, the police believed they had enough to charge the brothers with murder. The evidence included the thumbprint from the stamp on the package sent to Alick McKay which matched Arthur Hosein's. And experts also discovered Arthur's prints on a newspaper, which the kidnappers had dropped in the drive of the McKays' house on the night Muriel disappeared.

Arthur 'King Hosein' because of his assertion that he would become a millionaire. What they could not know was how he planned to realize his dream.

HOW THE PLAN WAS HATCHED

One night Arthur and his brother were watching TV when they saw Rupert Murdoch being interviewed. During the show, reference was made to Murdoch's wife Anna. Suddenly, Arthur had a plan.

He and Nizamodeen would find out where Anna Murdoch lived, abduct her and demand £1 million.The brothers did their homework, or so they thought, but made two errors. They got the addresses of Murdoch and McKay mixed up, and followed Murdoch's Rolls Royce, not realizing that Alick was using it while his boss was away.

All these facts were to emerge in court at the trial of the decade. Meanwhile, as

The brothers denied their guilt, however - and during police interrogation revealed very different characters.

Nizamodeen was almost child-like in his attitude to detectives. He once broke down sobbing on an officer's shoulder and cried: 'Oh my, what has Arthur done to me? What did Arthur say I was?'

Self-confident Arthur envisaged a film being made of the story - starring Richard Burton and Sammy Davis Jr

---

Arthur was a different kettle of fish altogether. He was articulate, and showed astonishing bravado. He even boasted that he would write a book about the case - the ensuing film would star Richard Burton as the officer in charge and Sammy Davis Jr as himself.

It was no use. At their trial at London's Old Bailey, Mr Justice Sebag Shaw jailed both brothers for life.

For months, police searched for the body of Muriel McKay. But the only people who know what happened to Mrs McKay are Arthur and Nizamodeen Hosein. And they have kept silent.

In a poignant postscript to the crime, Alick wrote in the *Sun* on the morning after the brothers were convicted:

One can accept death in the ordinary way...But in these circumstances, one is unable to accept the explanation of death without finding a body, although I am convinced Muriel is never coming home again. I must face this situation, of course, and face my life as best I can.

I suppose I do not want to know the brutal facts really, and yet I must always ask: How did she die? What happened to her? Where is her body?

Above: *Rook's Farm, Hertfordshire, where police searched for any sign of the remains of Mrs McKay.*

Below: *Dogs are employed in the search in the vicinity of Rook's Farm.*

LIZZIE BORDEN
The Mad Axe Killer?

It's one of the great unsolved cases in American criminal history. One sultry August day in 1892, did the browbeaten Sunday School teacher Lizzie Borden brutally axe to death the father and stepmother who made her life so miserable?

Lizzie Borden took an axe
And gave her mother forty whacks
When she saw what she had done
She gave her father forty-one

I t was a children's rhyme which was chanted in every school playground across the United States. Its echoes would haunt Lizzie Borden until the day she died. Had she, in blind fury, battered her hated stepmother to death, then done the same to her puritanical father? A judge and jury decided that she hadn't, and she walked free from court a wealthy young woman.

But if Lizzie was innocent, who was the Fall River Axe Murderer? The case remains one of the classic unsolved crimes in American history.

AN UNLOVING CHILDHOOD

Lizzie Borden was born in 1860 at 92 Second Street, Fall River - a cotton town in Massachusetts. And her relationship with her father was sealed at her birth. He had her christened Elizabeth Andrew, because he had wanted a boy.

Lizzie's mother died two years later and her father, Andrew J. Borden, married Abby Durfee Gray, a plain, plump, shrewish woman of thirty-seven. Mr Borden was a wealthy man, a former undertaker who had amassed close to half a million dollars in property deals. But he

Above: *Lizzie's mother had been dead for only two years when her father, Andrew J. Borden, remarried.*

Left: *Mrs Abby Durfee Gray Borden, who became Lizzie's stepmother.*

Opposite: *Lizzie Borden, whose father had given her the middle name Andrew because he had wanted a boy, not a girl.*

was also a miser.

Despite their wealth, the Bordens lived in conditions worse than many of the town's mill workers. Andrew Borden spent nothing on the shabby house in Second Street, even less on his children Lizzie and her elder sister Emma.

As Lizzie grew up she at first resented, then despised, her stepmother. She was

THIRD ST.

VIEW OF THE VICINITY OF THE MURDERS.

I. Borden house.
II. Borden barn.
III. The well.
IV. Fence with barbed wire on top.
V. Side entrance.
VI. Churchill residence.

VII. Dr. Bowen's house.
VIII. Dr. Chagnon's house.
IX. Kelley house.
X. Yard from which officers watched the Borden house.
XI. Kelley's barn.
XII. Pear orchard.

Above: *Second Street with the Borden home marked with the figure 'I'. Lizzie's father spent no money on their shabby home.*

convinced that the only reason she had married her father was to get her hands on his money. Lizzie refused to sit down for meals with her and always addressed her as Mrs Borden. Lizzie was plain, with curly red hair, quiet and introspective. She was an ardent churchgoer and her spare time was spent fishing, sewing - or just brooding at her bedroom window.

Despite the wealth he had accrued Andrew Borden was a miser, and his family lived in miserable conditions

---

It was in these unhappy surroundings that Lizzie Borden spent the first thirty-two years of her life. Then, on 4 August 1892, a single act of horrific violence destroyed the Borden household for ever.

THE DEED IS DONE

The little town of Fall River was in the grip of a severe heatwave. Lizzie's sister Emma could stand it no longer and moved out to the country to stay with friends at Fairhaven, twenty miles away.

Lizzie herself had been ill with food poisoning, and she had been brooding over two incidents which lately had made

her even more bitter. The first was when she discovered that her miserly father was going to spend some of his hoarded wealth - on her stepmother's sister.

Lizzie had flown into a furious rage and ransacked her stepmother's bedroom, taking some cheap items of jewellery. She claimed the house had been burgled, but it did not take long for her father to realize that Lizzie was the culprit.

The second incident had occurred in May when intruders broke into outhouses at the bottom of the Bordens' garden. Mr Borden's reaction was bizarre. He was convinced they had been after Lizzie's pet pigeons, so he took an axe to the birds and chopped their heads off.

Convinced that the intruders had been after Lizzie's pet pigeons, her father inexplicably chopped all their heads off

---

It was in this brooding frame of mind that Lizzie awoke on that fateful August morning. The family routine began as usual. After breakfast Mr Borden set off to check on his businesses. John Morse, his first wife's brother who was staying a few days, left to visit relatives. Mrs Borden began tidying and the servant, a good-natured Irishwoman, Bridget Sullivan, was cleaning the windows.

Just after 9.30am Mrs Borden was hunched on all fours cleaning the stairs leading to the spare bedroom. She was struck on the head and the body by nineteen blows from an axe. The first blow would have killed her instantly.

At 11am Mr Borden arrived back at the home, sweating from the heat. Lizzie made a fuss of him and left him dozing in the living room while she went into the kitchen to chat to Bridget. The maid then went upstairs to rest from the heat.

Ten minutes later she heard wild screams from Lizzie Borden. 'Come down, come down!' she yelled. 'Father's dead. Someone came in and killed him.' Bridget raced downstairs to find Lizzie guarding the living room door. She refused to let the maid enter, but ordered her to fetch Dr Bowen, the family doctor.

After a delay, the doctor arrived and examined the mutilated body of Mr Borden. He had been killed in exactly the

*Above: **The murder house, 92 Second Street, photographed in the late autumn of 1892.***

*Left: **Lizzie, it was revealed, had bought a bottle of prussic acid and a bottle of cyanide from the town's pharmacy.***

the fact that Lizzie showed no emotion. At the time she put this down to shock.

Mrs Churchill then asked Lizzie where her stepmother was, to which she replied: 'I'm sure I don't know, for she had a note to visit someone who is sick. But I don't know that perhaps she isn't killed also, for I thought I heard her coming in.' Mrs Churchill and Bridget took some minutes to find Mrs Borden's body, lying in a pool of blood on the stairs.

THE SUSPECTS LINE UP

At first, suspicion fell on John Morse, whose behaviour when he returned to the house had puzzled the crowd outside. He had been seen to slow down as he approached. Then, instead of going straight to the front door, he went round the back and picked some fruit from a tree. Police also thought he was a little too quick with his alibi. But when they checked it out it stood up well enough.

Detectives were convinced that the murders had to be the work of someone in the household. They soon eliminated Bridget Sullivan. She had no motive to commit such horrific killings: she was not mentioned in Andrew Borden's will, and there was no ready cash in the house.

That left Lizzie Borden. Her behaviour after the murders had been curious, to say the least. When Bridget had asked her where she was when her father was attacked, Lizzie replied that she had been out in the yard. But she told Mrs Churchill that she had been in the barn getting a piece of iron. When questioned by detectives she said that she was in the barn and had eaten three pears while she was there. Police combed the barn, but could find no trace of pear cores.

Lizzie said she had not seen the body of her stepmother as she came downstairs to greet her father. A neighbour told the police that the night before the murders Lizzie had told her that her father had enemies and that she feared for his life. But the detectives found no motive for murder among his business rivals.

It was also discovered that the day before the murders Lizzie had bought a bottle of prussic acid - cyanide - from the town pharmacy. She offered no explanation for this strange purchase.

same way as his wife. There were ten blows to his head, aimed mainly at his nose and eyes. Blood was splattered over the walls, the settee and carpet.

As Dr Bowen pulled a sheet over the corpse neighbours arrived at the house. One, Mrs Adelaide Churchill, did her best to comfort Lizzie, but was struck by

THE AXE-WOMAN ON TRIAL

In the weeks following the murders almost every newspaper in the USA tried and convicted Lizzie Borden. After all, it was a great story - spinster daughter takes bloody revenge on tyrannical father and wicked stepmother.

Detectives investigating the case tended to agree with the newspapers. Secretly they had drawn up a warrant for Lizzie's arrest, but they wanted to wait until after the inquest before it was served. They believed that Lizzie might give evidence at the inquest which would damn her.

The police were not disappointed. Lizzie Borden stood in the witness box and duly put her foot in it. She incriminated herself by stating that she had not been upstairs when her father had arrived home. It meant, of course, that she was trying to wriggle out of the awkward question of why she had passed her stepmother's body on the stairs without seeing it.

'I thought I was on the stairs but now I know I was in the kitchen,' she told the inquest. And she added confidently: 'Looking back on this dreadful event has made me recall things much more clearly.' After the inquest, Elizabeth Andrew Borden was charged with the first degree murder of Andrew J. Borden and Abby Borden, née Gray.

But by the time the case came to court the following June, small town America had rounded on the press for its shabby treatment of Lizzie. The God-fearing, clean-living daughter of a heartless father was now an object of public sympathy. In a complete turnaround, ordinary folk had decided that quiet Sunday School teacher Lizzie should not be standing trial for such a diabolical crime. Quite simply, she was innocent.

The police had a wealth of circumstantial evidence but hoped that Lizzie would give herself away at the inquest

---

Lizzie, meanwhile, had hit the jackpot with her choice of lawyer, George Robinson, a former Governor of Massachusetts. While in office he had appointed one of the three trial judges to the bench. At a pre-trial hearing this judge, at Robinson's request, decided to disallow any prosecution statements about the prussic acid episode. Lizzie's trip to the pharmacy was never mentioned in open court.

The trial lasted ten days, and as it progressed the prosecution's case began to look decidedly frayed around the edges. Lizzie helped her own cause by fainting in the dock, which brought a wave of sympathy from the jury.

COURTROOM BRILLIANCE

Robinson was brilliant throughout. He convinced the jury that the state had been callous in allowing such a put-upon, saintly girl to stand trial for a crime she could not possibly have had the heart or the stomach to commit. He finished his case for the defence by asking the jury: 'To find her guilty, you must believe she is a fiend. Gentlemen, does she look it?'

By the time of the trial public opinion had swung in favour of the God-fearing daughter of a heartless big businessman

---

The jury decided that she didn't, and pronounced her not guilty. Lizzie Borden stepped down from the dock and, to cheers from the public gallery, walked from the court a free woman.

And a rich woman too. She inherited most of her father's wealth, a sum beyond her dreams while he was alive. Despite the cruel chants of the children, Lizzie had no qualms about staying in Fall River, although she could not face living in the house which had brought her so much unhappiness. She soon moved to a house in a wealthy suburb.

Bridget Sullivan soon sailed back to Ireland, taking with her, it was said, a large amount of money generously donated to her by Lizzie out of her father's will.

For a while there were rumours that Lizzie and Bridget had hatched a plot together to rid themselves of the cruel old miser and his peevish wife. But the case was never reopened by the police. They appeared to be quite satisfied that they had arrested the true culprit, and that justice had run its course. The real killer, they were convinced, had been freed by a jury of twelve good men and true. The mad axe murderer of Fall River never struck again.

Left: Lizzie and her lawyer, former Massachusetts Governor George Robinson, during the trial.

Lizzie settled into her new house with her sister Emma, but according to neighbours they soon began arguing and Emma moved out. Lizzie Borden died a lonely spinster in 1927 at the age of sixty-seven, taking the secret of that hot August morning with her to the grave.

Today, the Axe Murders of Fall River still spark controversy. There exists in America a Friends of Lizzie Borden Society who regularly protest her innocence. But there are as many who are convinced that on that hot August day the downtrodden daughter of Andrew J. Borden finally snapped and wreaked her terrible revenge on those who had made her life a misery.

Below: The court house at New Bedford where Lizzie's ten-day trial took place.

OSCAR SLATER
Victim of Prejudice

Sherlock Holmes's creator had a mind as brilliant as that of his fictional detective - without it, the stories could never have been written. On one occasion Conan Doyle turned his powers of perception and deduction to a bizarre crime in the real world

More than a century after Sir Arthur Conan Doyle's gifted pen gave birth to Sherlock Holmes, the crime fighter and violin virtuoso remains fiction's greatest detective mind.

His enduring qualities of deductive reasoning, an eye for the minute and a skilled, analytical brain served him well throughout the amazing adventures he shared with his ever-loyal companion, Dr Watson. None of those who followed - not Poirot, Maigret or Ellery Queen - could equal him.

Almost from the very first appearance of Holmes, the public closely identified the author with his creation. From all over the world, letters poured in to Conan Doyle's home asking for his help.

Sir Arthur rarely accepted the implied challenge. There were a few exceptions, however, when the great writer felt a sense of outrage that justice had not been served and fair play thrown to the wind.

One concerned George Edalji, a vicar's son who happened to be a Hindu. Edalji was accused of a series of horrible animal mutilations around his village of Great

Above: *Scene of the crime - the dining room of 15 Queen's Terrace, a cushion by the fireplace showing the position of the body.*

Left: *An early picture of Miss Marion Gilchrist who was brutally murdered four days before Christmas in 1908.*

Opposite: *Oscar Slater strolls through London's Hyde Park shortly after his release.*

Far left: *Oscar Slater in 1908, the year he was accused of bludgeoning Miss Gilchrist to death.*

Above: *The hushed High Court in Edinburgh as Oscar Slater goes on trial.*

Above right: *Lord Guthrie, the High Court Judge who presided at Slater's trial. Slater was sentenced to death, but two days before he was due to be hanged his sentence was changed to life imprisonment.*

Wyrley in Staffordshire. Although he was of impeccable character and an established lawyer, the police, motivated by racism, got a conviction. Edalji was sentenced to seven years' hard labour.

Unfortunately Sir Arthur did not become aware of the young man's plight until three years later, in 1906. But within weeks he had gathered enough evidence to prove Edalji's innocence, and published his findings in the *Daily Telegraph* in January 1907.

Race hatred in the English Midlands sent a young Hindu lawyer to prison for crimes he had not committed

---

The articles had the desired effect. A commission was ordered to investigate Conan Doyle's claims, and Edalji was promptly released.

'He came to my wedding reception,' Sir Arthur recorded, 'and there was no guest whom I was prouder to see.'

THE CASE OF OSCAR SLATER

The second exception came soon afterwards - a series of events which Dr Watson might have recorded as 'The Case of the Ungrateful Dog'.

Like many of the Holmes stories it involved the bizarre, the fantastic and murder. In the end Conan Doyle's dogged investigation freed an innocent man,

Oscar Slater, from a wrongful life sentence with hard labour.

The story began just four days before Christmas, on 21 December 1908, with the brutal murder of Miss Marion Gilchrist. A reclusive, elderly spinster, she was found bludgeoned to death in her home at 15 Queen's Terrace, West Princes Street, Glasgow.

At first Conan Doyle was reluctant to get involved. But, as he later explained in his autobiography, 'when I glanced at the facts I saw...that this unhappy man had in all probability no more to do with the murder for which he had been condemned than I had.'

The eighty-two-year-old Miss Gilchrist seemed an unlikely victim for murder. She was a virtual hermit, and her only real pipeline to the outside world was her young maidservant, Helen Lambie.

On the night of the murder, Helen, twenty-one, left her mistress's residence to buy an evening paper. She would be gone less than ten minutes.

Miss Gilchrist, who had long been ill at ease with the noise and uncertainties of the world outside, made sure the locks of her double doors were securely fastened. Because of her advanced age, the lonely spinster had installed a latch on the outer door which could be opened by a long piece of string attached between it and her upstairs flat.

Returning with the newspaper, Helen found a frantic young man named Arthur

Adams outside Miss Gilchrist's door. Adams, a neighbour from a flat below, explained that he had heard a noise coming from inside the apartment, followed by a heavy thud. When he yelled out to Miss Gilchrist and got no answer, he came upstairs.

Helen unlocked the door with her key. Just as they were about to enter, a man appeared from inside. He approached as if about to strike up a conversation, then he suddenly brushed past them and fled.

Startled by the strange encounter, the servant and the neighbour cautiously entered the flat...and recoiled in horror as they found the body of Miss Gilchrist, her head brutally beaten and covered with a rug, sprawled out in the dining room in front of the fireplace.

The elderly spinster lay sprawled on a rug, battered to death - yet her valuable jewellery had hardly been touched

---

Despite her valuable jewellery collection, which was estimated to be worth more than £3000, all that was missing was a crescent-shaped diamond brooch worth some £50. However, a box of papers had been broken open and the contents strewn about, as if someone had been frantically searching for something.

Although Adams and Helen had both seen the man at close range, they were in some disagreement over his actual appearance. However, one thing later became clear: neither of the descriptions fitted that of Oscar Slater.

Adams immediately ran out to fetch a policeman, while Helen raced to the home of Mrs Margaret Birrell, Miss Gilchrist's niece. The maid blurted out that she had recognized the killer. But strangely Mrs Birrell rebuked her.

PREJUDICE CLAIMS A VICTIM

As word of the vicious killing spread, there was an immediate public outcry and the police were quickly put under intense pressure to make an arrest. Slater, a German-born Jew, was apprehended solely because he had pawned a diamond brooch of similar value to the one stolen just before embarking for America on the liner *Lusitania* with his French mistress.

The New York authorities were notified, and Slater was promptly seized and returned to Glasgow. Here, however, it was discovered that not only had he owned the brooch in question for many years, but that he had pawned it three weeks before the killing!

And yet both the public and the police refused to yield. They wanted blood and Slater, whose morals were shown not to have been of the highest standards, remained the only suspect.

The police then found a box of tools in his possession, and claimed he had used a small hammer to kill the elderly spinster. Never mind that Slater had a clear alibi - because his mistress and maidservant were his witnesses it was not allowed. Even the description of the killer was amended to resemble Slater more closely.

Slater's alibi was disallowed because its witnesses were his mistress and his maidservant

---

And so, in one of the greatest miscarriages of British justice, the hapless Slater was duly convicted in the High Court and sentenced to death. Then, just two days before he was due to be hanged, his sentence was commuted to life imprisonment.

Above: *Helen Lambie, the maid of eighty-two-year-old Miss Gilchrist and virtually her only connection with the outside world.*

Below: *Queen's Terrace (on the right) is where Miss Gilchrist lived and died.*

Above: *The body of Miss Gilchrist was found battered and covered with a rug, sprawled in the dining room in front of the fireplace.*

CHAMPIONED BY CONAN DOYLE

Slater would have spent the rest of his days in confinement, if he had not been championed by an indignant Conan Doyle. After an investigation which would have done Holmes proud, the author outlined the reasons why Slater could not have been the murderer in a brilliant pamphlet, entitled *The Case of Oscar Slater*.

'The trouble ... with all police prosecutions,' Conan Doyle wrote, 'is that, having once got what they imagine to be their man, they are not very open to any line of investigation which might lead to other conclusions.'

First, the author punched holes in the official motive of robbery:

When he [the killer] *reached the bedroom and lit the gas, he did not at once seize the watch and rings which were lying openly exposed upon the dressing-table. He did not pick up a half-sovereign which was lying on the dining-room table. His attention was given to a* wooden box, the lid of which he wrenched open. The papers in it were strewed on the ground. Were the papers his object, and the final abstraction of one diamond brooch a mere blind?

And yet, if it was indeed a robbery, ... it is very instructive to note his knowledge of their [the jewels'] *location, and also its limitations. Why did he go straight into the spare bedroom where the jewels were actually kept? The same question may be asked with equal force if we consider that he was after the papers. Why the spare bedroom?...Is not this remarkably suggestive? Does it not pre-suppose a previous acquaintance with the inside of the flat and the ways of its owner?*

But as Conan Doyle cleverly observed, there were limits to the intruder's knowledge. 'If it were the jewels he was after, he knew what room they were in, but not in what part of the room.'

Moreover, he suggested:

How did the murderer get in if Lambie is correct in thinking that she shut the doors? I cannot get away from the conclusion that he had duplicate keys. In that case all becomes comprehensible, for the old lady - whose faculties were quite normal - would hear the lock go and would not be alarmed, thinking that Lambie had returned before her time. Thus, she would only know her danger when the murderer rushed into the room, and would have hardly time to rise, receive the first blow, and fall, as she was found, beside the chair upon which she had been sitting.

Conan Doyle revealed how the police had misinterpreted the evidence and jumped to a hasty but illogical conclusion

---

The only other possibilities, he claimed, were that the murderer was actually hiding inside the flat when Lambie left, 'of which there is no evidence whatsoever', or that the intruder was someone whom Miss Gilchrist knew and who was therefore let in.

Next, Sir Arthur went over the evidence taken from the scene of the crime, his gaze as perceptive as that of

Holmes. He correctly pointed out that no blood was found on the wooden box, despite the bloody nature of the murder.

It has never been explained why a rug was laid over the murdered woman. It is at least possible that he (i.e., the murderer) used the rug as a shield between him and his victim, while he battered her with his weapon. His clothes, if not his hands, would in this way be preserved.

DOGGED PERSEVERANCE

Despite his conclusive and logical analysis, and his stinging rebuke of the Scottish Lord Advocate, the pamphlet still failed to win Slater's release.

But Conan Doyle waged a relentless newspaper campaign, and eventually an official government inquiry into the case was set up. Nothing came of it. Slater languished in prison.

It was not until November 1927 - eighteen years after Slater's conviction - that Conan Doyle's unyielding efforts proved successful. Slater was released pending a retrial. In June the next year he was pardoned - he was never exonerated - and given £6000 compensation.

Conan Doyle believed that the real murderer was a prominent citizen protected by the police

---

But if Sir Arthur had expected to meet a grateful citizen when Slater was pardoned, he was in for a rude awakening. Incredibly, he refused to repay the money that the author had put up as bail for his release before the retrial.

'He is not a murderer,' the author told a reporter, 'but an ungrateful dog.'

A MYSTERY UNSOLVED

The key question, of course, was never answered. To this day, the identity of Miss Gilchrist's murderer remains a mystery forever lost to the past. Helen Lambie kept her silence about the man she said she had recognized coming from the flat, and many people later believed the killer was a public person with a reputation to safeguard.

Sir Arthur was certain that was the case. Although he never publicly revealed his suspicions, shortly before his death he said he believed he knew who the real killer was: 'A man who was protected by the police because he was a prominent citizen who desperately wanted something from the private papers of Miss Marion Gilchrist. He has gone unpunished, but it is more important to me that an innocent man is free.'

It was never established just what secrets those private papers contained. But one thing is certain: they contained something to prompt a man to murder a helpless elderly spinster.

Left: *Oscar Slater in London in 1928, watching the pigeons outside St Paul's Cathedral.*

Below: *Cleared of murder ... Slater and his wife beside a Scottish river.*

D. B. COOPER
The Mystery Skyjacker

Skyjackers are reviled by most responsible governments, and feared by aircrews and passengers. So how did a mysterious American hold a plane to ransom and then pass into legend as a folk hero?

Not many skyjackers become heroes - but that was the way it happened for one of America's most mysterious criminals, the legendary D.B. Cooper, who bailed out of a passenger plane with $200,000 in cold cash to become an overnight folk hero!

Adored by millions who continue to sing his praises even to this day, Cooper nevertheless threatened to blow out of the sky more than 150 innocent men, women and children if the authorities didn't come up with the money. But the swashbuckling nature of the crime - and the fact that in the end no one was ever hurt - captured America's attention and turned this mysterious little man into a modern-day version of Robin Hood.

It was the perfect crime - and no one knew what had happened to the perpetrator

---

Indeed, it was the perfect crime...and to this very day, more than twenty years later, no one is really certain what ever became of him. Did he die in his brazen leap into the night? Did he succumb to a fatal disease? Or is he still alive today, living off his ill-gotten swag?

No one is sure how the bizarre story ends, but everyone knows how it began, quietly enough, on Thanksgiving Day, 24 November 1971, at Portland airport in the state of Oregon.

As hundreds of travellers milled around the departure lounge eager to get to their families and friends for the American national holiday, no one gave the quiet little chap clutching a canvas bag a second glance. He sat patiently amid the boisterous holiday atmosphere, seemingly a person of little consequence behind his dark-tinted glasses.

Almost an hour went by, but finally the 150 passengers who were taking Northwest Airlines' one-hour flight to Seattle were paged to begin boarding.

SHORT WALK TO FAME

D.B. Cooper - the name he had used to purchase his ticket - stood up from his seat in the departure lounge and began the short walk to the waiting Boeing 727. Still clutching the canvas bag, the only luggage he had brought with him, he worked his way down the cabin until he found his aisle seat - which was, as he had requested, opposite the place where the stewardesses would sit for take-off and landing.

The stewardess thought the passenger wanted a drink. Instead he handed her a note: 'I have a bomb with me...'

For the next twenty-five minutes, as the plane roared through the sub-zero temperatures towards Seattle, the man continued to play the part of a holiday-maker. But then, about halfway through the 400 mile flight, he pressed the button above his seat to summon a stewardess.

Tina Mucklow responded, thinking the man probably wanted a cocktail or a blanket. But to her horror he handed her a note, short but exact in its dire warning: 'I have a bomb with me. If I don't get $200,000 I will blow us all to bits.'

Mucklow was stunned as she read and reread the note. Then, without taking his eyes off her, Cooper opened the bag just wide enough so that she would know that this was no bad joke or bluff.

She could clearly see the intricate maze of dynamite sticks, wires and a detonator.

Then he closed the bag, and watched the shaken stewardess walk as calmly as

Opposite: *After warming by an early-morning fire, FBI agents resume digging for more of the $200,000 ransom beside the Columbia River.*

she could to the flight deck. It wouldn't be long now, he must have thought.

As soon as Mucklow delivered the quiet man's threat to the startled cabin crew the pilot radioed Seattle ground control, explaining the nature of their emergency. He couldn't have known, but within minutes a crack team of FBI agents, police marksmen and even local units of the National Guard were being deployed at key points around the airport. The authorities believed they were in for a long night of negotiations.

All that everyone, including Cooper, could do now was wait. For the next thirty-five minutes the Northwest jet proceeded to Seattle.

WAITING AT SEATTLE

As the plane made its way to the tarmac the pilot made a brief announcement to the passengers, explaining that there would be a delay in disembarkation. No reason was given, and the passengers reacted with understandable dismay.

As his fellow travellers talked angrily among themselves of missed connections and spoiled dinners, Cooper got out of his seat and, with the canvas bag still clutched tightly to his body, walked calmly up to the flight deck to face the pilot and his two senior assistants.

'Now, gentlemen,' he said quietly, without rancour. 'Don't bother to look around.' For the next twenty minutes there was a tense stand-off, as Cooper explained first to the air control tower staff, and then to a senior police officer, that his demands were inviolate: $200,000 in used bills and four parachutes in exchange for the safe release of all his hostages.

It wasn't until the released hostages were safely inside the terminal that they realized a skyjacking had taken place

---

The authorities knew they had no choice. They could not gamble with the lives of so many innocent people, who could be blown to bits if a rescue attempt was staged. Reluctantly, they despatched two FBI agents towards the captive jet.

Disguised as airport maintenance men, they wheeled aboard a trolley, containing a sack sealed with wire. Cooper opened it and, to his glee, knew he had won - the money and parachutes were inside.

Keeping his word, he then allowed the passengers to leave the aircraft. Incredibly, it wasn't until they were safely inside the main terminal and confronted by hordes of waiting reporters that they learned they had been the victims of a skyjacking, and that a man had threatened to snuff out their lives.

THE PASSENGER VANISHES

Meanwhile, as the passengers reacted first with surprise, then with shock, at their near-miss, back on the plane Cooper was preparing to put phase two of his carefully conceived plan into action.

With the flight crew still at the mercy of his bomb, he demanded that the plane be refuelled and then ordered flight plans to Mexico.

During his conversations with air traffic staff and ground crews, Cooper displayed such a knowledge of planes and airport procedures that authorities knew they were dealing with a smart, calculating supercriminal.

Once his demands had been carried out, Cooper ordered Captain Bill Scott to take the plane back into the night sky, where it was tailed by an Air Force fighter jet. But the skyjacker was a cautious, quick-thinking man who had apparently calculated the various responses the authorities would make.

In his instructions to the pilot Cooper revealed an intimate knowledge of flying and aerodynamics

---

As a result, not long after they were airborne he ordered the flight crew to change course. He never intended flying to Mexico, and instead told Captain Scott to head south - using detailed flight instructions that revealed an intimate knowledge not only of flying but also of the complexities of aerodynamics.

'Fly with the flaps lowered, 15 per cent,' he ordered. 'Keep the landing gear down. Keep the speed below ninety metres per second. Open the rear door and do not climb above 7000 feet.'

Once Captain Scott had got over the slight shock of realizing his captor was no ordinary criminal, he did some mental calculation regarding Cooper's specific instructions and informed him that they would cut heavily into their fuel supply.

Cooper calmly informed the captain he could land in Reno, Nevada.

Before leaving the cabin, he ordered the flight crew to keep the steel bulkhead door - which separated the cabin from the rest of the Boeing - locked for the remainder of the journey. He also ordered Scott to activate, as soon as he had left the cabin, the system which would open the rear door of the plane.

The captain complied, and the plane was suddenly engulfed by the deafening rush of thin, cold air.

For the next four hours, Scott and his crew flew by Cooper's instructions towards their ultimate destination. It wasn't until they had safely landed in Reno that they realized their passenger had literally vanished into thin air.

Cooper, wearing only light clothing, had parachuted out into rugged country in sub-zero temperatures. Was this his fatal mistake?

Later, a detailed examination of the plane's black box recorder would indicate a slight but perceptible altitude increase at 8.13pm - thirty-two minutes after the take-off from Seattle. Under cover of darkness and clouds, which hid him from view of the tailing Air Force jet, Cooper had leaped into the night, his ill-gotten booty strapped to his waist.

On the surface, it appeared to be the perfect crime. Not only had Cooper made a daring escape, but he had outwitted the combined efforts of the police, the FBI and the United States Air Force!

But after checking the black box recordings, officials realized he had made one terrible mistake in an otherwise flawless plan. When Cooper jumped, the Boeing had been flying over the inhospitable terrain of south-western Washington State - a rugged landscape dotted by deeply wooded areas.

Above: American newspapers reported in 1983 that Cooper was actually a Missouri conman. It was just one of many 'leads' that led exactly nowhere.

Moreover, the temperature would have been below zero that night, and Cooper had been dressed only in lightweight clothes and shoes, a raincoat his sole protection against the bitter elements. Further, he had no food.

The odds against him surviving the leap were overwhelming.

The terrain was so hostile that ground searches quickly became bogged down, and the authorities were instead forced to rely on wave after wave of aerial searches in the two weeks after Cooper's incredible disappearing act. But even planes equipped with heat sensors turned

Above: *FBI agent Himmelsbach who was specially assigned to the Cooper case. Not even the FBI, however, were able to track down the phantom skyjacker.*

would be romantic, or heroic, or any of the other euphemisms that seem to attach themselves to situations of high risk. I don't blame people for hating me for what I've done, nor do I blame anybody for wanting me caught and punished, though this can never happen. I knew from the start I would not be caught. I have come and gone on several airline flights since and I'm not holed up in some obscure backwoods town. Neither am I a psychopath. I have never even received a parking ticket.

A FOLK HERO IS BORN

The letter caused a sensation. Cooper may not have considered himself a hero, but the public did.

Letters and phone calls poured into newspapers and radio stations across the country praising his slick escapade. T-shirts bearing his name became as trendy as those espousing 'Peace and Love'. And hundreds of young women pledged themselves to be his bride - that is, if he could ever be found.

But not everyone was enamoured with Cooper - a frustrated FBI reportedly held back from the public a psychiatric mental profile, fearing it would only bolster his swashbuckling image.

Moreover, not everyone was convinced that it was he who had written the letter. Many of the woodsmen who were at home in the hostile terrain over which Cooper had jumped openly labelled it as the work of a crafty con man.

When part of the rear door of a 727 was discovered, a 'Gold Rush' of excited treasure-seekers turned up

---

They believed that Cooper had been killed in the jump, or soon afterwards by the elements, and continued their hopeful treasure hunts across the wild landscape. So too did thousands of holidaymakers who went on 'Cooper's Loot' weekends - though they were attracted to the area more for the scenery and the barbecues than for any serious treasure-hunting.

As fortune-seekers - earnest and amateur - poured into the region where Cooper had gone down, the authorities

up empty, and people began to wonder if the high-flying thief would surface again.

Then, suddenly and without warning, three weeks after the skyjacking, a mysterious letter arrived at the offices of the *Los Angeles Times*.

'I am no modern-day Robin Hood,' the letter began. *Unfortunately, I have only fourteen months left to live. The hijacking was the fastest and most profitable way of gaining a few last grains of peace. I didn't rob Northwest because I thought it*

continued their aerial reconnaissance for traces of the elusive skyjacker and his ill-gotten booty. They, too, doubted the validity of the *Times* letter, and believed he could not have survived the jump.

But all the searches came up empty and finally, twelve months after the skyjacking, the FBI publicly announced that they believed him to be dead. Four years later, on 24 November 1976, the Bureau officially closed its file on the Cooper case.

Under the statute of limitations, the only crime he could possibly be charged with by then was tax evasion - assuming, of course, that he was still alive.

That was the last time most people thought they would ever hear of the mysterious D.B. Cooper...and for several years they were correct.

But in 1979, a hunter stalking deer came across a tattered plastic sign which read: 'This hatch must remain firmly locked in flight.' It was the warning sign from a Boeing 727 rear door hatch. The discovery caused a sensation, and treasure-seekers by the thousands began to pour into the dense forests where the sign had been found.

COOPER'S LOOT

Despite their efforts, however, the missing loot remained undiscovered.

Then in 1980, a full nine years after Cooper's dramatic escapade, father and son Harold and Brian Ingram were walking along the muddy bank of the Columbia River north-west of Portland when the eight-year-old boy noticed a wad of old, sun-bleached $20 bills.

There was $6000 in all, which the authorities believed had been washed down the river from the higher terrain to the north.

When the money was handed over, officials checked the serial numbers against those of the bills given to Cooper. There could be no mistake - the money was part of Cooper's cache.

To many, the discovery proved beyond a shadow of a doubt that Cooper had indeed died in his daring parachute jump, and that his loot had been scattered to the four winds. The Ingrams' discovery sparked yet another bout of interest in

Cooper's Loot by locals and out-of-towners, who came pouring into the region once more in hope of suddenly striking it rich. But again they were foiled. No more money was ever found.

Then, in 1989, a skin-diver seeking clues to Cooper's fate found a small parachute in the Columbia River about a mile upstream from where the money had been located.

Despite the immediate frenzy the discovery caused - even after so many years had gone by - it was eventually determined that the parachute was not connected to the Cooper case.

With the parachute and the money weighing him down, did Cooper drown in the icy Columbia River?

Earl Cossey, the man who had helped pack the original chutes demanded by Cooper, said it bore no resemblance to those given to the skyjacker, and because of its small size he thought it might have been used for a flare. It could even, he felt, have been a child's toy.

The diver who found the parachute was working for Californian lawyer and former FBI agent Richard Tosaw, who has spent every Thanksgiving for the past ten years searching for Cooper's remains.

Tosaw, who wrote a book titled *D.B. Cooper, Dead or Alive*, says he believes the skyjacker drowned, and that his remains got caught up on one of the rows of pilings that extend into the river about every half-mile to prevent erosion.

'He didn't know where he was when he baled out,' said Tosaw. 'He hit the water with the parachute on his back and the money packs around his waist, and went down. He is still down there somewhere. So is the rest of the money, snagged on an old rock or stuck in the mud.'

Despite his annual searches, however, Tosaw, like hundreds of other treasure-seekers before him, has come up empty-handed each time. None the less he vows to continue the hunt.

D.B. Cooper's most elusive secret remains just as enigmatic as it did twenty years ago - and the chances are that it will never be solved.

WHITE MISCHIEF
Who killed Lord Erroll?

Cocaine, champagne and adultery were the hallmarks of the rich and pleasure-seeking Happy Valley set in 1940s Kenya. This was the background for a crime of passion committed by a jilted husband who saw his whole world crumbling

Not since the Romans frolicked with Bacchanalian abandon did a ruling caste indulge in such wanton displays of hedonistic pleasure. The white elite which lived in splendour among the breathtaking natural beauty of Kenya's White Highlands, a place nicknamed Happy Valley, abandoned themselves to pleasure in all its forms.

COCAINE, BOOZE AND SEX

They reached their zenith in what was then a British colony during the years of World War II. As their compatriots at home endured the privations of rationing and separation, the gilded set of Happy Valley partied at a feverish pitch.

Drunken, sexually depraved cocaine snorters, the Happy Valley residents cared little for the world's woes as long as their frivolous existences were not menaced by Hitler or the taxman.

Happy Valley's residents cared little for the world's woes so long as their own frivolous existences were not menaced

---

Near to the Wanjohi River, not far from the capital, Nairobi, the first white settlers in Kenya had been drawn to the magnificent White Highlands by the fertile soil which yielded high-grade coffee and tobacco. But any frontier spirit

Above: *Sir Henry Delves Broughton was thirty years older than his English rose of a wife, Diana.*

Opposite: *Among the flowery 'bright young things' at Ascot racecourse in 1937 was Lady Diana Delves Broughton.*

that may have existed in Victorian times had been washed away by the expats who inhabited these beautiful hills during World War II. This 'little England' had become an enclave for laziness and lotus eaters whose idea of a tragedy was too little ice for their sundowners at the Muthaiga Country Club.

No one was more suited to this meaningless existence than Josslyn Hay, a philanderer and a rogue. Hay was the Earl of Erroll and High Constable of Scotland, but he forsook the rigours of the Scottish Highlands for those of Kenya. Expelled from Eton, cited in an English divorce court where the judge branded him 'a very bad blackguard',

the war and the rest of his idle life in Kenya. As it was he was murdered - undoubtedly for his philanderings.

But to this day his killer's identity remains a secret, although more than a few fingers have been pointed to the grave of Sir Henry Delves Broughton.

Sir Henry was the exact opposite of Josslyn Hay. True, he was aristocratic, privileged and drank too much. But he had two attributes alien to Hay - honour and a wife. The wife, Diana, was an English rose beauty who at twenty-six was thirty years younger than him.

Sir Henry - known to all his friends simply as Jock - was suffering financially in England, the legacy of bad business judgement and even worse judgement on the racecourses. Ancestral homes in England had been mortgaged and Kenya was seen as his last great chance to recoup a fortune by raising cattle.

But he still had sufficient funds to enjoy a splendid lifestyle in Happy Valley, and he felt certain that his young bride would appreciate the social whirl.

'I saw her eyes boring into me and I knew then I must have her'

Within weeks of his arriving in Africa Josslyn Hay met Diana for the first time, on 30 November 1940, at the Muthaiga Club. Hay would later say to friends: 'Never can I remember a woman having such an immediate impact on me. I saw

Hay arrived in the cushiest of wartime foreign postings as British military secretary in Nairobi.

He had commented to a friend in England before his departure: 'Not much chance of catching a bomb there, what?'

Had it not been for a certain meeting, a certain knowing smile, it might well have been that Josslyn Hay would have sat out

Above: *Josslyn Hay, the Earl of Errol, who was murdered, undoubtedly because of his infidelities.*

Below: *The Muthaiga Country Club, where the Happy Valley set liked to meet, drink and flirt.*

her eyes boring into me and I knew then I must have her. I walked over to her while Jock was at the bar and said: "Well, who is going to tell Jock, you or I?" '

Diana found his dangerous sensuality electrifying. Both of them were willing participants in the passion.

THE MISERABLE CUCKOLD

It was said that Hay derived as much pleasure from seeing cuckolded husbands squirm as he did from bedding his sexual conquests. Diana was no exception.

Hay began to flaunt her mercilessly in front of their friends, including of course Jock. He twirled her around the dance floor, their embrace lingering too long, their clinches too tight for anyone to mistake what was passing between them.

Poor Jock, muttered friends with some shreds of morals left. But the kindly old man bore his humiliation with British stiff upper lip stoicism.

In January 1941 he found a letter addressed to him at the club. It read: 'You seemed like a cat on hot bricks last night. What about the eternal triangle? What are you going to do about it?' Several days later, when Diana left for an 'all girls' swimming party, another note informed him that there were no girls on the outing. Just Josslyn Hay.

Hours after Jock received the last note, Diana returned from her trip and told her husband she was leaving him.

Desperate to keep his wife, Jock said he would tolerate Diana's affair if she kept up the pretence of marriage

---

It is a measure of the man that he told her then that he was willing to put up with the relationship provided she continued to live with him. He offered her a three-month cruise to Ceylon.

Diana declined the offer of the cruise, and two days later walked out on Jock with a £5000 set of pearls which he offered as an inducement to stay.

What this trauma did to the balance of Jock's mind has been the subject of

Above: *Happy Valley's dwellers enjoyed all that privilege and position could bring them. The dashing young Earl of Errol (in the back row, wearing a bow tie) was one of their leading lights.*

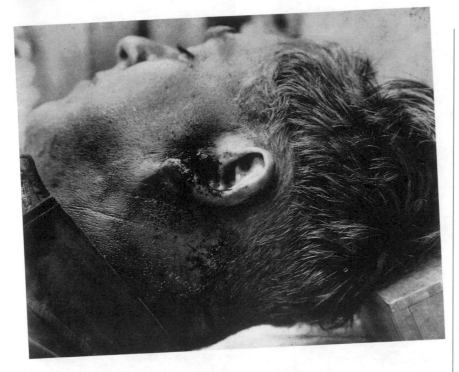

Above: *The Earl of Errol,
who was shot in the head in
the free-living paradise
community known as the
Happy Valley.*

gentility, even going so far as to inquire of Hay how the war was going. The tea party was followed by evening carousing, during which Jock raised his champagne glass at the Muthaiga Club and said: 'I wish them every happiness. May their union be blessed with an heir. To Diana and Joss.'

Less than three hours later Hay was dead in his car which had careened off the Nairobi-Ngong road. There were three neat bullet holes in his head.

THE MURDER

When the police later reconstructed the bizarre events of that night, they discovered that Jock had wheedled from him a promise that Diana could spend one last night under her husband's roof.

It transpired that Jock had staggered to bed, inebriated, at 2am and was sound asleep at 2.15 when Hay's American Buick purred through the wrought iron gates of his ranch and dropped Diana off.

It then left the road two and a half miles from Jock's mansion and plunged into a gravel pit. At 3am two labourers found Hay. Two hours later Jock was woken by police, who broke the news.

Jock, of course, was the chief suspect. He had both the motive and the means to commit murder. Within twenty-four hours the police had found near his home bullet casings that matched those found near the murder scene.

**The Happy Valley set thought Diana
was against her husband. Instead she
hired a first-class lawyer for him**

While his wife slept, Jock went into town to see the corpse of her lover. Then in the afternoon he piled numerous personal effects into a pyre and set them alight. Only one item remained, to be found two days later - a charred, bloodstained sock that led police to their conclusion: the cuckolded husband had killed his rival and burned the clothes splashed with the victim's blood.

The Nairobi CID had formulated a theory which went like this. Far from being sozzled on champagne, Jock had merely feigned inebriation. He had then

speculation ever since. His staff who served dinner for him that night reported that he seemed pensive. Perhaps he was plotting the next move in the tragedy - which came the next day.

On 21 January he called the local police to say that two revolvers - Smith and Wesson service-issue models - had been stolen by burglars who had broken into his study.

After making a statement to the police he visited a lawyer to see about getting a divorce, and then wrote a painful letter to a friend back in England. He said: 'It is a hopeless position...I think I will go to Ceylon. There is nothing for me in Kenya any longer.'

It was painful but true; as well as losing his wife, his cattle venture had fared badly, losing him £10,000 in the first few months.

**At June Carberry's tea party the
cuckolded Jock was charming to his
rival Hay**

Some of his friends rallied around poor old Jock. As Diana moved into Hay's home, Mrs June Carberry, who despised Jock's wife, invited him to a tea party to try to cheer him up.

Unfortunately, at the last moment Diana and Hay turned up too. Jock gave a command performance of civility and stolen out of the house and lain in wait on the lonely road for Hay to come by.

They lowered Josslyn Hay into the ground on 25 January, but it was not until 10 March that charges were laid against Jock. More surprising, however, was Diana's flight to South Africa, where she hired the eminent Johannesburg lawyer Harry Morris to defend her husband.

CIRCUMSTANTIAL EVIDENCE

Jock performed magnificently in court. Observers felt a groundswell of public gallery sympathy, as Morris laid bare the philandering, cocaine-taking antics of this gilded but tarnished set.

Jock walked free on 1 July 1941. Morris had sent the ammunition from the murder scene to ballistics experts in London, who ascertained that the bullets could not have come from a Smith and Wesson service-issue revolver.

Jock was free, but his life destroyed. His relationship with Diana survived long enough for her to share the cruise to Ceylon. But halfway through it Jock fell badly and hurt his back, and transferred

Right: *Sir Henry Delves Broughton and his wife Diana at Sandown Park racecourse in 1939.*

Below: *Sir Henry Delves Broughton and the first Lady Broughton (born Vera Boscawen) with their son Jock at Derby racecourse in 1928.*

to another steamer to take him to England. Diana continued on the voyage and then made her way back to Kenya.

Jock, with nothing left to live for, committed suicide in Liverpool in 1942.

One of the witnesses at his trial had been June Carberry. She testified that she too had been staying in his house the night the killing was committed, and swore that he was too drunk to do anything other than flop on to the bed.

Did Jock Broughton confess all to a sympathetic fifteen-year-old schoolgirl?

But now, aged sixty-five, her daughter Juanita has come forward with a startling claim - that Jock confessed all to her when she was a schoolgirl. She said: 'He told me: "I hate Happy Valley and its people." I felt a great loyalty to him and I don't think he was wicked or a criminal...I know he killed him.'

Perhaps in the end the only person who really knew what had happened was Diana. Was it possible that she sensed, one day, that she too would be discarded when Hay's fancy turned to another woman? Was it possible that she took his life to spare herself that dreadful day?

Maybe. But Diana died in 1987 and the secrets of those days died with her.

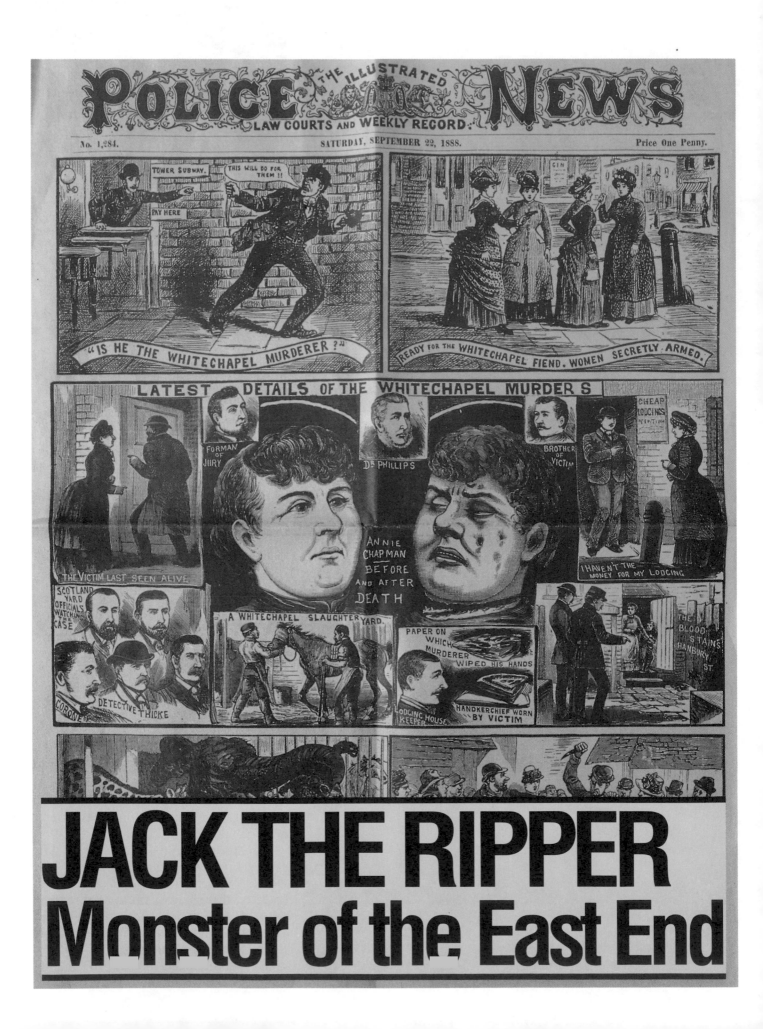

In 1888 London's East End saw a series of brutal murders of prostitutes which remain unsolved today. Was Jack the Ripper a maniacal surgeon?
A Jewish ritual slaughterer?
An insane member of the royal family?

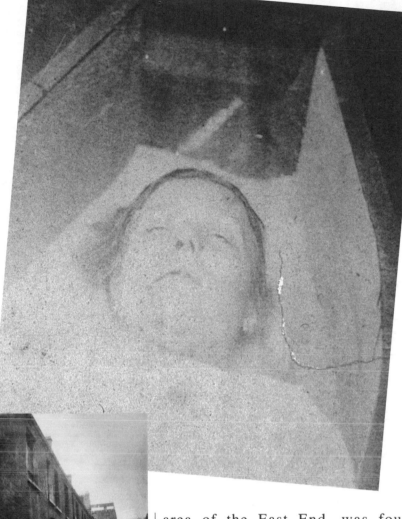

In 1888 the British Empire was at its zenith. The lands ruled from faraway London spanned the globe, embracing peoples of every race, creed and colour.

But in the centre of this huge domain there was a place where the sun never shone. The East End of London was a disgrace to the empire and to civilized values. People lived there in poverty and squalor. Child deaths were double the national average. Prostitution and drunkenness, sexual abuse of minors, murders and muggings were all rife.

This was the sordid environment for a killer whose notoriety lives to this day. Jack the Ripper made the mean streets of the East End his killing ground.

His crimes were not that remarkable, given the catalogue of horror man has come to terms with in the twentieth century. He only murdered five women - admittedly in a gruesome manner.

But it is the question of identity, with all the lingering suspicions that Jack the Ripper may have been someone highly placed in British society, which has made the 'Monster of the East End' an immortal creature of intrigue.

THE FIRST VICTIM

Jack the Ripper may have gone down in history as an infamous murderer but his reign was in fact short. He first struck on 31 August 1888. Mary Ann Nichols, a prostitute who haunted the Whitechapel

Top: Mary Ann Nichols, a prostitute known as 'Pretty Polly', was the first victim of the horrific 'Monster of the East End'.

Above: The street where the body of Mary Ann Nichols was found lying across the gutter.

Opposite: A contemporary newspaper relates the Ripper story in a particularly lurid fashion.

area of the East End, was found butchered in the labyrinth of dark alleys.

'Pretty Polly', as the forty-two-year-old whore was known, was a chronic drunkard and a well-known habituée of the area's gin palaces.

Fourpence provided a whore with a doss house bed for the night and a few swigs of cheap gin

---

Police believe she had approached a tall stranger with the time-honoured 'Looking for a good time, mister?' She would have requested fourpence for her services, enough for a doss house for the night and perhaps a few tumblers of gin.

By the time the man had dragged her into the shadows it was too late. A hand went round her throat, and in seconds she was cut from ear to ear.

'Only a madman could have done this!' said a police surgeon later. 'I have never seen so horrible a case. She was ripped about in a manner only a person

Top: *'Dark Annie'* *Chapman, already dying of tuberculosis, was disembowelled.*

Above: *One of the letters sent to the police - possibly from Jack the Ripper.*

Although there was no obvious sign of rape, with this murder - as with the first - there was every indication that the killer had been motivated by some terrible sexual rage as he cut and slashed. The dissection of Dark Annie, with all her entrails laid next to the corpse, indicated a knowledge of anatomy or surgery not found in the the average sex killer.

GRUESOME SEQUEL

The second murder had an extraordinary sequel. On 28 September a mocking letter was sent to a Fleet Street news agency. It read:

I keep on hearing that the police have caught me. But they won't fix me yet. I am down on certain types of women and I won't stop ripping them until I do get buckled. Grand job, that last job was. I gave the lady no time to squeal. I love my work and want to start again. You will soon hear from me with my funny little game. I saved some of the proper stuff in a little ginger beer bottle after my last job to write with, but it went thick like glue and I can't use it. Red ink is fit enough I hope. Ha! Ha! Next time I shall clip the ears off and send them to the police, just for jolly.

It was signed: 'Jack the Ripper'.

The way the bodies were disembowelled indicated a knowledge of anatomy or surgery on the part of the murderer

---

A later letter, sent to the Whitechapel Vigilance Committee, was accompanied by half a kidney. The sender claimed it was from a murder victim - and that he had eaten the other half.

No one can be sure that the writer of this second letter was the same as the author of the first. But it is known that the Ripper removed some of the victims' organs. After expertly slitting their throats he would set about gruesome mutilations, slashing open faces and abdomens, ripping out intestines. Some he would arrange around the bodies, others he would take away.

The Ripper's third victim was Elizabeth Stride, nicknamed 'Long Liz' because of her height. On 30 September a

skilled in the use of a knife could have achieved.' Yet despite the horror, murders in that deprived and depraved area of London were not uncommon, and the police were happy to put this one down to a single, frenzied attack...until one week later.

On 8 September 'Dark Annie' Chapman, a forty-seven-year-old prostitute dying of tuberculosis, was found butchered near Spitalfields market.

rag-and-bone cart driver alerted police to a suspicious bundle. They found the body of forty-four-year-old Liz near factory gates in Berner Street, Whitechapel.

Like the others, her throat had been cut from behind - but she had not suffered mutilation or sexual savagery. This led police to think that the Ripper had been disturbed in his grisly work. For on the same day they found victim number four a few streets away in Mitre Square.

THE SPATE OF BUTCHERY CONTINUES

Catherine Eddowes, in her forties, was disembowelled and her face practically hacked off. Her intestines were draped across her right shoulder and both her ears were missing.

By the time of the fourth murder, Ripper hysteria had gripped London. Women began arming themselves with knives and carrying whistles to attract the police. *The Illustrated London News* rather fancifully suggested that ladies should now carry pearl-handled pistols in case the Ripper was tempted to move up the social scale. One shop even advertised steel corsets. Lower down the social order, in Whitechapel itself, policemen took to dressing as prostitutes in an attempt to decoy and trap the killer.

In one rare moment of farce a constable was accosted by a journalist, also dressed in gaudy women's clothing, and asked: 'Are you one of us?' The policeman replied: 'Certainly not' - and arrested him.

Half a human kidney accompanied a letter signed 'Jack the Ripper' - the other half, said the sender, he had eaten

---

The Eddowes murder disturbed the police greatly. Her body was the worst mutilated of all the victims. From her corpse there was a trail of blood leading to a torn scrap of her apron in a doorway. And nearby on a wall was scrawled in chalk the message: 'The Jewes are not men to be blamed for nothing.'

Sir Charles Warren, head of the Metropolitan Police force, personally removed the message, and may thereby have destroyed vital evidence. He was

Below: Mary Kelly, just twenty-five years of age, was grotesquely mutilated in her squalid home. The previous night she had been accosting strangers, asking for money.

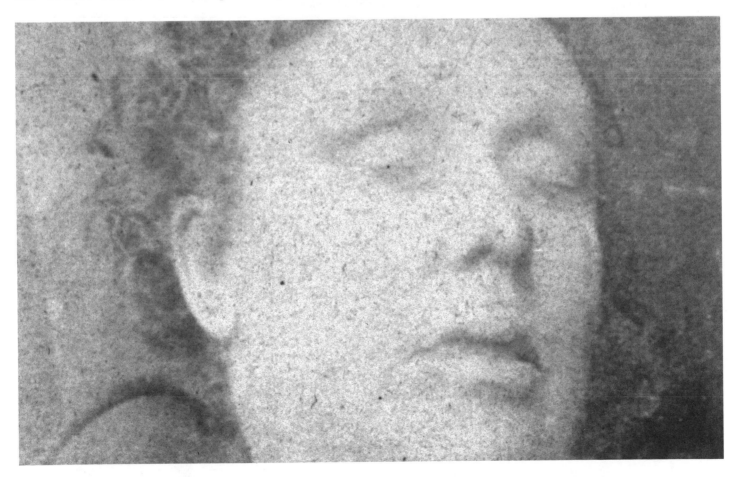

concerned that, with the influx to the East End of Jews from eastern Europe, the inscription could lead to savage reprisals.

RUMOURS AND SUSPECTS

The rumours about who the killer could be spread like wildfire. Some of the frightened wretches who lived in the area said it was a policeman on his beat.

Another suspect was a Russian-born doctor called Michael Ostrog, rumour having it that he had been sent by the tzarist secret police to stir up hatred against expatriate Jews.

Others said it was a mad surgeon. Blame even attached to Sir Charles Warren himself - a leading freemason who had supposedly removed the notice to protect a masonic killer.

The final death came on 9 November. The only difference this time was that the victim was a better class of prostitute; she had a room of her own.

Mary Kelly, twenty-five years old, was grotesquely mutilated in her rented home. This time the Ripper had been able to spend many hours at his grisly work.

On the morning of the 10th, her landlord Henry Bowers knocked on her door to collect unpaid rent. The previous evening the attractive blonde had been accosting strangers for cash. The last one she approached - tall, dark, with a moustache and deerstalker hat - was her killer. Later it was discovered that the woman had been three months pregnant.

Her death was to be the last. Yet, a century and more later, the puzzle of the Ripper's brief but bloody reign had still not been solved.

' there she was, all her entrails steaming hot. She had red and white stockings on'

In 1959, seventy one years after the killings, an old man recalled driving a cart down Hanbury Street on 7 September, 1888 and hearing the cry 'Murder!' He said: 'I jumped off, being a lad, and joined the crowd...and there she was, all her entrails steaming hot. She had red and white stockings on.' That was the second victim, Annie Chapman.

Above: *Rumours were rife about who the Ripper could be. One eye-witness described Mary Kelly's last client (and therefore probably her killer) as tall, dark and with a moustache.*

One suspect who has continued to cause violent debate is Queen Victoria's grandson, Prince Albert Victor, Duke of Clarence. The finger of suspicion was pointed at him because he was said to be mad - and after the killings was supposedly incarcerated in a mental institution for fear of the scandal.

The Duke was the eldest son of the future Edward VII, and was said to be a bisexual who turned insane after catching syphilis. But police claimed he was either at Balmoral or Sandringham on the nights of the murders.

But perhaps the number one suspect is Montagu (some reports spell his name

Montague) John Druitt, whose body was found floating in the Thames a few weeks after the murder of Mary Kelly.

In their book *The Ripper Legacy*, authors Martin Howells and Keith Skinner say that Druitt, an impoverished barrister, was the man whom the police of the day reckoned to be the guilty party. Druitt's family, it was claimed, had a history of mental illness, and Druitt himself had been trained in medical skills as a young man.

JILL THE RIPPER?

Another author, William Stewart, suggested that Jack the Ripper was really Jill the Ripper, a midwife and illicit abortionist jailed as a prostitute who took a terrible revenge when released.

Top cop John Stalker, who retired in the late 1980s as Deputy Chief Constable of Greater Manchester, delved into the Ripper files and declared:

Was the Ripper Queen Victoria's grandson, turned mad by syphilis?

There is still not a shred of real evidence against anyone sufficient for a court of law. The truth is that Jack the Ripper was never in danger of capture. The police, I am certain, came nowhere near him. The Metropolitan Police of 1888 were dealing with something quite new - the first recognized series of sexual murders committed by a man who was a stranger to his victims. And a hundred years on, those are still the most difficult crimes to investigate.

And yet one man who has delved into the Ripper files more than anyone else believes firmly that a culprit for the murders was identified.

John Ross is an ex-policeman, now curator of the Metropolitan Police's so-called Black Museum at New Scotland Yard. Not a man noted for jumping to conclusions, he tells visitors to his grisly exhibition that Jack the Ripper was an immigrant named Kosminski, of whom little is known beyond his surname.

Mr Ross believes that all the on-the-spot police work at the time pointed to this suspect. And he is not alone.

In February 1894 a predecessor of Mr Ross with the same analytical mind, Sir Melville McNaughton, wrote a seven-page memorandum which was added to the Ripper file in an attempt to silence some of the wilder theories being postulated at the time.

Former top policeman John Stalker says Ripper-type cases are still the most difficult to solve

---

His notes read: 'Kosminski, a Polish Jew and resident in Whitechapel. This man became insane owing to many years' indulgences in solitary vices. He had a great hatred of women, especially of the prostitute class, and had strong homicidal tendencies. He was removed to a lunatic asylum around March 1889. There were many crimes connected with this man which made him a strong suspect.'

Below: *Millers Court, Dorset Street, in the East End of London - typical of the squalid spots where Jack the Ripper committed his grisly crimes.*

NAZI TREASURE
Division of the Spoils

A series of brutal murders, all of old people, in a small community. Not Agatha Christie, but the work of someone determined to keep an old wartime secret. It all stemmed from the Nazis' lust for riches...

The ringing of the doorbell roused Salvatore Leonardi from his armchair in front of the television at ten o'clock on a Sunday night. It was unusually late for a friend to be calling. Something was clearly amiss. Why else would anyone walk up the dirt track to his home, perched on a hill overlooking the village of Bargagli in northern Italy?

Leonardi pushed himself out of his chair and walked to his back door. Opening it, he found himself staring into the barrels of a sawn-off shotgun.

It is unlikely that his eyes had time to focus on the face of his visitor, for both barrels were emptied before the door had swung fully back.

The killing was inexplicable to the police who descended on the village after the crime in September 1989, and no one in the small community seemed willing to enlighten them. Even Leonardi's widow could provide no clues to the murder of a silver-haired retired barber.

'My husband...was a calm man,' she said, 'who led a quiet life and enjoyed looking after his chickens and his rabbits. But my husband said many times recently that he would not live long.'

The mayor of Bargagli was unwilling to discuss the murder. He also said: 'I don't want to get involved. We don't discuss these deaths in this town.'

The reason for his remarks was that Leonardi was not the first villager to have been murdered by the night stalker who had become known as '*il mostro di Bargagli*' (the monster of Bargagli). The

Above: *Neuschwanstein Castle near the Swiss frontier where the US Seventh Army found a huge hoard of loot stolen by the Nazis from private collections.*

Right: *An American soldier examines an item of Goering's stolen art treasury.*

Opposite: *Invaluable paintings are removed from Neuschwanstein Castle.*

assassin had claimed twenty-one victims - seventeen men and four women - and the only clue to his identity was his age. He must have been an old man...having first struck forty-four years earlier.

AMBUSHED BY THE PARTISANS

For it is in 1945 that the answer to the mystery lies. In February that year, three months before the liberation of Italy, a Nazi convoy carrying banknotes, gold, and possibly jewellery, paintings and other looted works of art, was ambushed

Above: *Hermann Goering planned to build a vast art gallery in Linz, to be named after himself and to be handed over to the Third Reich on his sixtieth birthday.*

Right: *As an art connoisseur and an ex-art student himself, Hitler (seen here with Prince Paul of Yugoslavia) knew the value of Europe's art treasures.*

by Bargagli partisans in the nearby Tecosa valley. The SS guards escorting the loot back to Germany were wiped out by machine-gun fire and the 'Treasure of the Tecosa' disappeared without trace.

Carmine Scotti, a policeman detailed to investigate the disappearance of the loot, was found days later horribly tortured and roasted alive on a spit. He was to be the first link in the chain of victims attributed to '*il mostro*'.

A local policeman ordered to investigate the disappearance of the treasure was found roasted alive on a spit

---

'*Il mostro*', whoever he or she may have been, was determined to ensure that the whereabouts of the treasure remained a secret. Within two months of Scotti's death there were eight more killings. In April 1945 four partisans, thought to be meeting to share out part of the treasure, were machine-gunned to death. Two days

later four more partisans perished, this time the victims of a bomb.

The villagers, it appeared, had fallen out over the spoils of war. But the murders quelled any dissent. Clearly '*il mostro*' had suppressed the opposition within the partisans' ranks, because during the next sixteen years peace prevailed in the village.

A few of the villagers had by then built new houses from apparently freshly generated wealth, but no one asked questions and police interest had petered out. It was not aroused again until 1961.

THE MONSTER RE-EMERGES

In December that year Giuseppe Musso, a seventy-two-year-old gravedigger and former Bargagli partisan, fell from a bridge into a ditch and fractured his skull. It was dismissed as an accident.

The death of Maria Balletto, sixty-four, at her home in the village in December 1969 was certainly no accident. The old lady, a former despatch rider for the partisans, had been bludgeoned to death.

The killings continued. In November 1972 Gerolamo Canobio, aged seventy-six, drank too much one night and shouted out that he was going to reveal the secret of the missing treasure. Hours later he was found dead, his skull smashed in with a rock.

A distinct pattern was emerging. All the victims were elderly and had fought with, or had strong links with, the partisans during World War II - the sort of people who might know the answer to the riddle of the missing Nazi loot.

The next to die was seventy-four-year-old Giulia Viacava, a former freedom fighter whose head was smashed in by a stone in March 1974. Two years later

Pietro Cevasco, aged fifty-four, was found hanged by his own belt from a tree.

Carlo Spallarosa, sixty-nine, met a still more horrific death in June 1978. He was decapitated when he 'fell' down a cliff.

Some villagers actually survived attacks but remained silent ever after. Francesco Fumera, seventy-five, was shot at close range with a sawn-off shotgun in 1980 but later insisted he had not seen his assailant.

In July 1983 the story took a bizarre new twist. It revolved around Anita de Magistris, the widow of the German officer who had led the ambushed convoy - and who had survived the attack.

In 1974 'the Baroness', as she became known, suddenly moved to a villa on the outskirts of Bargagli. Surely she had returned to try to trace the treasure.

As the years passed she became integrated into the community, a regular churchgoer who led the parish choir. But at least one villager was concerned by her continued presence. In July 1983 'the Baroness' was killed by a series of blows to her head with a heavy stick or club.

A woman magistrate, Maria Rosa d'Angelo, was drafted in to investigate the murders. One woman who appeared willing to help her was Emma Cevasco, aged seventy-seven. But shortly before she was due to give evidence she fell to her death from a second-floor window.

Fearful for their own lives, the villagers had been too scared to give evidence

D'Angelo concluded that the villagers had been immobilized by fear. 'This may explain the seeming indifference of the local population,' she said.

The silence that kept the village's treasure safe has done the same for secret hoards throughout Italy and beyond. For the story of Bargagli is just one small chapter in the mysterious saga of the Nazi fortunes - first looted, then left as the Germans retreated across Europe.

As the threat of conflict grew in the late thirties, Europe's moneyed classes, Jews and non-Jews alike, began to panic. How could they keep their homes and riches safe from the Nazis?

It didn't take the Nazis long to realize that easy pickings were slipping through their fingers. Hitler ordered the formation of a shady organization - headed by his ruthless right-hand man Martin Bormann - called *Sonderauftrag Linz* (the 'Linz Special Mission'), which was in effect a legalized band of thugs and thieves.

The Fuehrer now ordered special vaults to be constructed to house the various fortunes. Once his armies moved west, the vaults were quickly filled as Bormann's human vultures extorted and stole. New treasure chambers were still under construction when the most valuable prize of all fell - art-rich Paris.

The race to loot the French capital was obscene. Hermann Goering, head of the Luftwaffe, built his own personal fortune by diverting trains of art treasures to his private estate at Karinhall, near Berlin.

Apart from the national heritage of France, the Nazis stole all they could lay their hands on in a spree of trans-European crime. More than half the national wealth

Above: *Rudolf Hess addresses a Nazi rally. Chiefly famous for his dramatic flight to Britain in 1941, Hess was also the nominal boss of Martin Bormann, one of Hitler's henchmen in the rounding-up of loot.*

defeated Nazis formed a new, secret organization with the title ODESSA.

ODESSA was set up with the aim of finding secure escape routes and fresh identities for the German war criminals. A fortune was spent. But there was still a greater fortune left over...

WHAT HAPPENED TO THE REST?

During the final assault on Berlin in May 1945, a bizarre bank raid took place as American forces raced their Soviet allies to reach the centre. The target was Berlin's Reichsbank - and its contents.

To this day nobody knows who got the bulk of the booty. But it is believed that, of the American share, £200 million in gold and securities went missing.

Intelligence services on both sides of the Iron Curtain believed that after the war about £50 billion of gold alone remained unaccounted for. Much of it may still be hidden in Europe.

In their flight, many of the Nazis found the sheer weight of their booty too heavy to transport. Billions of pounds' worth was dumped by the roadsides of Europe.

In 1983 workmen renovating the well of a monastery in northern Italy found the shaft blocked by heavy metal chests. When they were raised, they were found to contain 60 tons of gold, worth well over £500 million at the time.

An embarrassed Italian government admitted that their wartime allies had removed 120 tons of gold from Rome's central bank in 1944 and had loaded it on to trucks to take back to Germany.

How much actually reached the Fatherland no one knows. Some may have been stolen by the Germans, some abandoned. Some may have been ambushed by Italian partisans...

Which brings us back to Bargagli, and the string of grisly murders culminating in the shooting on his doorstep of poor old Salvatore Leonardi in September 1989. Whatever secret Nazi treasure he was protecting, it failed to protect him.

As one farm worker of Bargagli said in 1989: 'Some terrible things happened during the war and some terrible things are still going on. It's as simple as that.'

of Belgium and Holland vanished. Polish and Czechoslovak bank vaults were stripped. In Russia, 50 trains a month returned to Germany with the contents of museums, art galleries and banks. By the time the tide of war had turned, the Nazis had plundered an estimated £15 billion worth of treasures - worth inestimably more at present values. But as Allied bombers ripped the heart out of German cities, the greedy Nazis realized that their loot was not safe.

Some of the ill-gotten bullion was hidden in salt mines near Alt Aussee in Austria. Diamonds were stored in a monastery in Czechoslovakia. Outside Füssen in Bavaria lay a treasure-store castle, Schloss Neuschwanstein. So much is known. But a great part of the hoard just vanished. Again, this can be put down to Teutonic efficiency. For the

Above: *Martin Bormann tried to bully Swiss bankers into handing over the accounts of clients whose money could go into the coffers of the Third Reich.*